Where Do the Paga

Just about every ethnic and cultural group today has some form of personalized, valid history that attests to the achievements and glory of that people, to promote a special sense of ethnic, national, racial or religious identity.

Until now, the historical origins of Paganism have been ignored or misrepresented by Western religious historians. The time is ripe for a new perspective, for an uncensored history of Paganism, an older concept of religious belief that—unlike mainstream Western religions—is not dominated by an orthodoxy held in power by threats of damnation or by law.

Dancing Shadows sheds light on the ancient origins of religion to give Neo-Pagans a sense of where they belong in its history, and how Pagan and mainstream beliefs have interacted over the centuries. This is an evocative, readable account written by a degreed historian who has studied and researched religious history independently for many years—and who has also been a Pagan for over twenty-five years.

The Christian and Judaic faiths dominate western society and our perspectives on the nature of religion, social development, and cultural values—but these faiths are relative latecomers in the overall history of religious belief. It is time to realize the interconnectedness of people and beliefs and to aim for cooperation based on the reality of our shared experience of being human on this planet. *Dancing Shadows* will convince you that the true source of continuing religious conflicts is irrelevant today, and that the only way to true religious freedom is through knowledge of the past and hope for the future.

About the Author

Aoumiel has been a solitary practitioner of the craft for over 25 years. The ambiguity of religion toward the purpose for life, the worthiness of women, respect for the Earth, and the fate of billions of people labeled as "unsaved" led her to seek elsewhere for answers to the questions often left unaddressed or confused in Christianity. To that end, she directed her studies to history, combining therein the subjects of language, religion, art, and archaeology, as well as events. Her early studies and natural inclinations led her to the practice of Natural (or Green) Wicca. For her, the Craft is both intuitive (both her mother and maternal grandmother were "Craftwise") and learned, and she has found a connectiveness with Wicca that she felt was missing in other belief systems. She is married, has a daughter and son, and teaches at the high school level in a conservative state.

To Write to the Author

If you wish to contact the author or would like more information about this book, please write to the author in care of Llewellyn Worldwide and we will forward your request. Both the author and publisher appreciate hearing from you and learning of your enjoyment of this book and how it has helped you. Llewellyn Worldwide cannot guarantee that every letter written to the author can be answered, but all will be forwarded. Please write to:

Aoumiel
c/o Llewellyn Worldwide
P.O. Box 64383-691, St. Paul, MN 55164-0383, U.S.A.
Please enclose a self-addressed, stamped envelope for reply, or $1.00 to cover costs.
If outside U.S.A., enclose international postal reply coupon.

Free Catalog From Llewellyn Worldwide

For more than 90 years Llewellyn has brought its readers knowledge in the fields of metaphysics and human potential. Learn about the newest books in spiritual guidance, natural healing, astrology, occult philosophy and more. Enjoy book reviews, new age articles, a calendar of events, plus current advertised products and services. To get your free copy of *Llewellyn's New Worlds of Mind and Spirit*, send your name and address to:

Llewellyn's New Worlds of Mind and Spirit
P.O. Box 64383-691, St. Paul, MN 55164-0383, U.S.A.

Llewellyn's World Religion and Magic Series

DANCING SHADOWS

The Roots of Western Religious Beliefs

Aoumiel

1994
Llewellyn Publications
St. Paul, Minnesota 55164-0383, U.S.A.

FIRST EDITION
First Printing

Cover art by Lissane Lake
Cover design by Linda Norton
Editing and interior design by Connie Hill
Photographs by the author

Library of Congress Cataloging-in-publication Data
Aoumiel
    Dancing shadows : the roots of western religious beliefs / Aoumiel.
        p.   cm. — (Llewellyn's world religion and magic series)
    Includes bibliographical references and index.
    ISBN 0-56718-691-2 (soft): $12.00 ($12.50 Can.)
        1. Indo-Europeans—Religion 2. Dravidians—Religion. 3. Europe—Religion. 4. Indus River Valley—Religions. 5. Witchcraft—History.   I. Title.
II. Series.
    BL660.A58   1994
    200'.9182'1—dc20
                                                                    94-15702
                                                                    CIP

Llewellyn Publications
A Division of Llewellyn Worldwide, Ltd.
P.O. Box 64383, St. Paul, MN 55164-0383

Llewellyn's World of Magic and Religion Series

At the core of every religion, at the foundation of every culture, there is MAGICK.

Magick sees the world as alive, as the home which humanity shares with beings and powers both visible and invisible, with whom and which we can interface to either our advantage or disadvantage—depending upon our awareness and intention.

Religious worship and communion is one kind of magick, and just as there are many religions in the world, so are there many magickal systems.

Religion and magick are ways of seeing and relating to the creative powers, the living energies, the all-pervading spirit, the underlying intelligence that is the universe within which we and all else exist.

Neither religion nor magick conflict with science. All share the same goals and the same limitations: always seeking truth, forever haunted by human limitations in perceiving that truth. Magick is "technology" based upon experience and extrasensory insight, providing its practitioners with methods of greater influence and control over the world of the invisible before it impinges on the world of the visible.

The study of world magick not only enhances your understanding of the world in which you live, and hence your ability to live better, but brings you into touch with the inner essence of your long evolutionary heritage and most particularly—as in the case of the magickal system identified most closely with your genetic inheritance—with the archetypal images and forces most alive in your whole consciousness.

Acknowledgements

To the people who have had the courage to write openly about Witchcraft and Neo-Paganism, and to the historians and archaeologists who have dared to face the criticisms of mainstream religions in publishing the findings that contradict orthodox beliefs.

To my family for their unconditional support.

To my husband, in particular, for his contributions in discussions and research.

Dedication

This book is dedicated to the Goddess and the God, and to the Elementals for their love and assistance in keeping me on track.

TABLE OF CONTENTS

ILLUSTRATIONS

Author's Note

When I was a child, my parents gave me a party favor they had received at a New Year's Eve celebration. The item was a ball of colorful paper ribbon. When I shook it, I could hear something rattle at the ball's core. I saw at once that this pretty little sphere could be unraveled, or it could be kept and treasured with its secrets intact. I admired the colorful ribbon-like windings trimmed in a golden foil. It was a thing of beauty to my childish eyes. And yet—there was the rattle.

I chose to unravel and seek out the secret, knowing full well that once done, it could not be rewound. But daring anyway to satisfy my curiosity and live with the consequences, I sat down on the floor and pulled the strip of paper. I discovered to my delight that as I unwound the ball, small favors popped out—a little tin dog, a plastic heart, a shiny star—each one to be carefully inspected and admired before I proceeded to uncover the next item. Then at last, I came to the end of the search, the paper ribbon ball all unwound to show that at its heart was a tiny metal whistle. I lined up my prizes on the hardwood floor along with the wad of pretty paper and blew my whistle exuberantly.

In many ways, that is how this investigation got started. Many years ago, I looked at the colorful ribbon and foil-wrapped ball called religion and saw that it was very attractive. I shook it and it gave a faint rattle. Some people, I know, are content to hold the prettily wrapped sphere and do not seek out the heart of the package. They gaze at it, handle it, and keep it close—or put it on a shelf except for special occasions. I could leave well-enough alone and always have my secure little ball to look at, but then I would never know what lay at its center. I knew that once I began to unravel the ribbon, the ball would never be quite the same again; but unless I did unwrap it, I would not make discoveries and acquire knowledge. I chose to unravel it.

As I peeled the ribbon away, once again, little prizes fell out. This time I found the jewels of beliefs and saw that the deities worshipped by different peoples were like the baubles of my childhood—each one an individual in its own right, and each one with its own charm and admirers, but none of them the core. I continued to explore until, at last, I located the center and what lay hidden therein. To my surprise and gratification, I discovered along the way that others had made this same trek and were drawing conclusions similar to my own. I feel that I have found a new perspective from which to view the history of religion, and it is the fact that the searches of others have made so little imprint in the area of general knowledge that inspired me to write this book and share my findings. It is this treasure that I now lay before you, the reader.

Introduction

The title of this book alludes to a philosophical story the author read long ago, "Allegory of the Cave," attributed to Socrates. Essentially, the tale describes a scene wherein a group of people live at the bottom of a huge cavern. They see shadows of creatures dancing on the cave wall and believe these images are deities. One of their number breaks the local taboo and scales the cave wall only to discover that high above is a ledge inhabited by another group of people. These people have a bonfire going and are parading deity animal silhouettes around the fire, and whenever they pass, the images are cast to the cave wall seen from below. Like the people at the lowest level, they too believe that they possess all the knowledge they need to have, but the hero continues to break taboos—this one against leaving the cave—and departs. To his amazement, he discovers more people and the living animals represented in the silhouettes. When he returns with his news to the people of the upper cave level, they disbelieve him and toss him to the lower level. When he tells his people there what he has encountered, they throw stones at him. The student is then left to explain the allegory, which here is treated in the sense that people will worship the reflected images of religions, but will refuse to accept the reality from which these images are derived. Modern mainstream religions are giving worship to the dancing shadows of an earlier concept, and the author is using her Craft name to avoid the stones.

NOTE ON DATING

Years ago, historians began using a new dating system, one that reflected their realization that the Bible did not deal with historical events, and thus could not serve as the marker by which all history should be written. To persist in the use of B.C. (Before Christ) and A.D. (Anno Domino—"Year of Our Lord") only served to both support a particular religious group while ignoring others, and to blur the line between history and mythology. As a result, the initials B.C.E. and C.E., which shall be used in this work, began to be seen in history writings in the late 1960s. The meaning varies according to the source and may be read as Before Common Era and Common Era, Before Current Era and Current Era, or Before Christian Era and Christian Era, although the latter is not a typical usage.

The reader is free to chose whichever interpretation is more comfortable.

The First Great Civilization

Many historians and scholars, among them, John Marshall, Josef W. Hall, Jacquetta Hawkes, Will Durant, Cottie Burland, Alain Danielou, Charles Picard, and Anne Ross, believe that the earliest known civilization came not from Mesopotamia or Egypt, but from an area larger than either—from the Indus Valley. Situated across from modern Oman at the north end of the Arabian Sea, the cities of the Indus were the source of inspiration for those developing in the Near East, and trade between these regions included not only goods, but gods.

The Indus culture, which predates the Egyptian, Babylonian, and Sumerian cultures, is known as Harappan (after the northern-most city in the valley, which, although it was built after Mohenjo-daro in the southern region of Sind, survived the longest) or Dravidic (a name so ancient no one knows where it came from, but Klaus K. Klostermaier in his book, *A Survey of Hinduism,* traces it from an Indian ethnic group back to the original inhabitants of the Indus), and it is the latter name that will be used herein. The Indus civilization stretched from the Himalaya Mountains to the Arabian Sea. Hawkes notes that some historians have theorized that the vast expanse was actually two regions united by a highly centralized government, with the major cities being Harappa in the north, below the Himalayas in the region called Punjab, and Mohenjo-daro in the south in Sind. However, a third city has been recently discovered, and this, along with some 70 other settlements in the area of Sind, indicates that rather than capital cities in north and south, there may have been a network of cooperative cities and towns, or city-states.

Seals typical of Mohenjo-daro have been found in Sumeria, and the early Indian cobra symbols, the naga, have been incorporated into the seals of early Mesopotamia. A. L. Basham states in *The Wonder That Was India* that the Sumerian references to a land called Melukka are believed to refer to the Indus Valley. Sumeria imported goods from the Indus, but did not export to the valley, which is a classic colony arrangement. The Indus has a vast history as a manufacturing center, and, like England exporting goods to colonial America, the Indus may well have been the parent of colonial Sumeria.

Historian Gordon V. Childe went so far as to describe the Mohenjo-daro of 4000 B.C.E. as having a Golden Age that would compare to that of Athens under Pericles, and certainly to any town of Medieval Europe. Childe concluded that there is sufficient evidence to declare that the most ancient Near East civilization, that of the Sumerians, came from the Indus as a colony, and this would make the Indus Valley the true "cradle of civilization." Sir John Marshall, archaeologist and historian, agreed and called the Indus the oldest civilization known. The announcements by Childe and Marshall startled the Western world, according to Durant, and the educated elite began intensive studies into the history, philosophy, and theologies of India, but the information apparently never filtered down from the learned journals and treatises into the school systems. Currently, the conclusions being drawn from archaelogical evidence are that Knossos was also a colony of the Indus, to become what Danielou calls a sister-civilization to Mohenjo-daro, and the colonies showed parallel development in their cultures.

Hawkes, in *The First Great Civilizations*, describes the Indus as a place where two races of people lived and worked together in apparent harmony without any trace of class or race distinction.

The more primitive humans were originally found in Punjab and later intermixed with the people of Sind. They were a taller race, considered to be "proto-Australoid," with long heads, low foreheads, and pronounced brow ridges, whose descendants may still be found in the jungle tribes of Central and Southern India. These proto-Australoid people are believed to be representative of humanity's most ancient race, according to S. S. Sarkar in the study, *Aboriginal Races of India*. Cottie Burland's article, "Africa, South of the Sahara" in the compilation, *Primitive Erotic Art,* takes this a step further and sees the Kalahari Bushmen and Pygmies as related to these Indus people. The other people, who were more common in the Dravidian culture of South India, seem to have been of a Mediterranean background, with a slighter build and higher forehead.

The excavations at Mohenjo-daro show a highly urbanized civilization with a strong social and economic foundation. The city is so ancient that no one has dug down far enough to find the peak of this culture, much less its beginnings, for as the excavations go deeper, the cultural artifacts become more refined than what had been previously uncovered, indicating that the actual height of this culture still remains undiscovered.

Unfortunately, earlier levels of the city lie below the current water table, so the foundations are still undated. Yet even after its peak, this city of the Indus (and Harappa appears to have been built exactly like it) had sewers underneath the streets with earthenware pipes and public drains of brick that were accessible by inspection holes (the first manholes of history), indoor bathrooms (complete with standing baths and seated toilets—unlike those of the Orient that are today still typically floor toilets requiring the user to squat), public baths, houses with central courtyards, and streets that were carefully planned to be straight in a north/south and east/west pattern with crossings at right angles. This kind of city planning and authority, complete with sanitation inspectors and workers, simply did not exist in other regions. Even at its latest, less powerful phase, the Indus civilization was ahead of anything produced by Babylon.

The people of the Indus had an agricultural society based on the first known example of large scale irrigation, which the Northern Aryans destroyed during their invasions and then later wrote about in the Rig-Veda ("Holy Scriptures" or "Holy Hymns," circa 1000–500 B.C.E.). Popular tradition holds that "Aryans" means "Noble Ones." However, Sir Monier-Williams in 1893 suggested that the derivation came from "area," for open space, and hence nomads, or "peasants."

The Dravidians had cotton cloth when no one else did; had abundant gold which they mined and dredged from the rivers; grew wheat, barley, peas, rice, sesame, mustard, melons, and dates; domesticated numerous animals including pigs, sheep, camels, horses, elephants, cats, and dogs; made fine porcelain pottery; were excellent woodcarvers; made decorative ornaments; and had the first known minted coinage. Examples of metalwork are very rare, prompting some historians to conclude that they were not very skilled at it and turned to wheel-thrown pottery instead. This may be simplifying the matter overmuch, for the riches of the Indus were legendary in Mesopotamian and Chinese writings long before the Aryan invasions began in the outlying regions of Sind, circa 2150 B.C.E., and reached the cities, circa 1500–1200 B.C.E. It may be that the Aryans, who wrote in the Rig Veda of the riches they found, simply took all they could and melted down the loot. This would be a better reason for the lack of metal artifacts in the Indus, for those few metal items of the Indus culture that have been found possess a remarkably lifelike and animated quality.

Archaeological evidence shows that the Indus Valley has been inhabited since at least 470,000 B.C.E. By 30,000 B.C.E., cave paintings in Sind were depicting people with scimitars, swords at their waists, bows and arrows, double-headed drums, and both wild and domesticated animals, whereas European cave paintings did not come into existence for another 10,000 years (20,000 B.C.E.), and those do not show swords and daggers. Indeed, A. L. Basham states that 10,000 B.C.E. is typically given as the beginning of civilization, as indicated by domestication of animals and cultivation of crops, but that was before Bhimbhetka. The cave paintings discovered in 1967 at Bhimbhetka (*The Indian and Foreign Review*) never made it into the *National Geographic,* because throughout that year this important window into the history and culture of the world was concentrating on Biblical themes, discussing the Holy Land of Palestine where Jesus walked, and the locales of various Old and New Testament Bible stories. This narrow view of Western people—the exclusion of anything that detracts from the Biblical version of human history—is one reason why information about the true origins of religion has for so long eluded the grasp of the general public.

The paintings at Bhimbhetka can be seen as further evidence that metalworking was not unknown, and lend support to the hypothesis that the lack of metalwork or weaponry at the later sites of Mohenjo-daro and Harappa may have been due to the thoroughness of the Aryan conquest. The overall picture that develops from this area prior to the invasions is one of a peaceful and cooperative community in which the rural areas and the urban centers acted in accord for mutual benefit. The grain was gathered into huge storage buildings in the cities and food was distributed from these central warehouses. Farmers used horse- or bull-drawn carts with two solid wooden wheels to take their crops to the granaries, and some crops, metalwork, woodcarvings, and other trade goods were shipped by boat to the Arabian Peninsula. Artifacts of the Indus have been found in Babylon as well as the more ancient Sumeria (modern Iraq), and merchants from Sind lived in Ur and other cities of Mesopotamia.

By tracing language, it is possible to see the extent of Indus influence in history. Danielou, in *Gods of Love and Ecstacy: The Traditions of Shiva and Dionysus,* writes that the Dravidic language and culture had spread to the Mediterranean, leaving traces in the surviving cultures and languages of the Basques, Georgians, and Baluchistanis. The Sumerian language is seen as related to Dravidic, as are the languages of the Lydians, Etruscans, and early people of Crete. The Dravidic-based languages of the Pelasgians of Southern Italy were referred to by Herodotus in his *Histories* as barbarian and related to the Etruscan and Lydian languages—in other words, not of Aryan descent. The same appellation is given to the language of the people of Malta in 69 C.E. by the Apostle Paul when he was shipwrecked there. R. F. Willets notes in *Cretan Cults and Festivals* that the language of early Crete and Greece is non-Greek and was found throughout the southwestern part of Asia Minor before the advent of the Aryan tribes of Acheans and Dorians, while Danielou adds that the still-spoken Dravidic language of southern India has not been considered by linguists yet as an aid to deciphering the ancient Mediterranean languages. The bias against changing the focus of civilization away from the Near East is strongly engrained by the Judaic-Christian tradition.

Objects from the Indus have been found at Troy and in Palestine, and the connection between the Indus Valley and Crete has been noted by a number of scholars, including Mortimer Wheeler (in his work, *The Indus Civilizations*), Durant, Danielou, Gaetano de Sanctis, and Paolo Santarcangeli. The Minoan Civilization of Crete contains the elements of the Indus worship of Shiva, with bulls, snakes, phallic images, horns, circular domed funeral chambers built like those of the Indus, and Yoga positioning of the dead (as is still done in modern India among the Shivaites). The Minotaur is a creature of Shivan background, a guardian, and can be seen in Shivan temples in India. Danielou believes that the Achaean Aryans conquered Crete around 1600 B.C.E. (Durant, writing 40 years ago, makes it 1900 B.C.E. for the first destruction of the palaces of Crete) and took the Minoan religion of Shiva to the Peloponnese Peninsula, and from this came the basis for the Mycenaean culture.

The Indus boats had a design with high prows and a single mast, rather like Viking boats would later appear, and Indus merchants are known to have visited Sumer and Akkad. By 1500 B.C.E., however, when the Aryans began their intensive assaults on the major cities of the Indus, trade slacked, then stopped altogether. It is clear that the cities, particularly Mohenjo-daro, continued to trade with Mesopotamia until the Aryans finally overwhelmed them in 1200 B.C.E. By the time the Aryans had fought their way from the

Bhimbhetka Cave and Rock Drawings

outlying regions of Sind, taken the smaller towns and villages, and finally attacked the cities, citadels of fired brick on top of 40-foot high mounds of mud-brick were in existence and fortified with towers and walls. The rhomboid-shaped strongholds contained massive granaries, and the indication is that the people knew there were invaders working their way across the land and that they had time to prepare for a long siege.

In all the Indus cities and communities, there is no sign of any temple structure. These people were reputed to have been unusually tolerant of varying ideas, and loved to discuss conflicting concepts. Hawkes states that they kept shrines in their homes, but had no centralized clergy and no priesthood. Each person was responsible for his/her own worship, but artwork indicates that the community would gather for special occasions marked by agricultural schedules, solstices, and moon phases. Sadly, the streets and houses of Mohenjo-daro give mute testimony to the final stages of that great city. Archaeologists have unearthed the skeletal remains of those who did not flee in time from the Aryans but were cut down, their bodies left in the streets or huddled together in the houses were they were slain. It was for them that the city was named, for Mohenjo-daro means "City of the Dead."

The Rig Veda of the Aryans recounts the tale of their hero, Indra, and his chariot-driving warriors conquering the contemptible, but rich, dark-skinned people who lived in fortified strongholds. He destroyed the forts and the irrigation canals, took the wealth of the Indus, and established Aryan rule over what is now modern Pakistan, India, and Bangladesh. The oldest civilization of humankind fell during Egypt's Empire period and was forgotten for 3,000 years, until rediscovered in 1924 by Sir John Marshall's Indian aide, R. D. Banerji; yet Greek and Indian texts speak of the early westward expansion of the religion of Shiva, and Diodorus refers to the travels of the Egyptian Osiris (whom Danielou and others connect with Dionysus) to India. The religion of Shiva covered a vast expanse, and had moved from Sind to Portugal by the sixth millennium B.C.E. Danielou believes it inspired the megalithic monuments and menhirs of Malta, Europe, and the British Isles, built circa 3000 to 2000 B.C.E. The importance, then, of the Aryan invasion of Sind cannot be stressed enough in terms of religious development in the Western world.

The Near East religious centers originally practiced the religion of Sind, and it was not until the Aryans realized that the religion they had imposed on the Indus people had become infiltrated with the religion of the Dravidians that religious orthodoxy became an issue. It was this need to return to a purer Aryan system that resulted in the rise of Judaism, Christianity, Islam, and the Holocaust of World War II. The discoveries in Sind have been recounted in a number of history books, yet are barely mentioned, if at all, in public school texts. Why this condition exists is based on the shattering of previously accepted Bible truths and the local control over texts given to people who are led by ministers. Books that deviate from accepted Bible history are simply rejected. Even Will Durant could not elude tradition as he states that the earliest coins of humankind came from the Indus, circa 2900 B.C.E., but this is given in a footnote discussing how the coinage of Lydia under Croesus set the example for the Mediterranean world between 570–546 B.C.E.

At the time of the discovery and early excavations of Mohenjo-daro, British archaeologists were stunned at what they were uncovering; but the British Empire was already in serious trouble in India, and while the news of this great civilization continued to trickle into the West, it was not as important as the information of two world wars and the social, political, and economic upheavals already in evidence. A number of prominent historians have written the truth about the mythic basis of the Old and New Testaments of the Bible, but even today, these myths are presented as genuine historical fact in public school textbooks, while history is ignored or labeled as myth. An entire chapter in one high school world history book is devoted to the story of Moses, the Passover, and the Exodus, although modern archaeology has shown that these events never took place. The possibility of correcting this situation is brighter now than it has ever been in the past. Perhaps this book will help pave the way for serious changes in the way people look at the role of religion in society and public education.

The proper place to begin in rediscovering the roots of religious beliefs is with the earliest known evidence of worship and the deities around whom this worship was/is centered. The surprising thing is that the first known worshipped God and Goddess of humankind have continued to be the objects of veneration to over 660 million people today. They can be traced into the religions of Mesopotamia, Egypt, Greece, Rome, and Europe; from ancient times to modern times, they have made their indelible mark on religious development in one way or another. These deities are dated back to at least 28,000 B.C.E. and are Shiva and Shakti, the God and the Goddess of the Dravidic Indus Valley, and of modern Hinduism. It will not be necessary to discuss the complexities of Hinduism in depth here to cover the relationship between these earliest deities and modern religion. Instead, the progression of events will be the guideposts to a nontraditional view of history and religion.

By 28,000 B.C.E. the God Shiva was being depicted in cave paintings as the Lord of the Beasts, with horns on His head and animals all around Him. He is seated on a low stool in what is now considered a Yoga position, with the soles of the feet touching, and He is ithyphallic (depicted with an erect penis). Here is the God familiar to the Old Religion of Europe in His earliest known portrayal; as erotic ascetic, a god of life, fertility, wisdom, and the hunt. But He is not alone. His partner is literally His other half, for Shiva is also portrayed in ancient times as half male and half female. His female aspect is Shakti, the Goddess of Power compared to the God of Grace. She is Uma, by which name She was worshipped in Mesopotamia, and She is the Mother Goddess, sometimes shown as pregnant or holding an infant in Her arms, and the Corn Goddess. "Wheat" is the American word for the European term "corn," but historians generally use the European word, while the American word "corn" should more properly be called "maize." Typically, all references in history texts, and in this book, to Corn Mothers, Corn Maidens, Corn Dolls, and so forth, unless addressing American her-

itage, are speaking of wheat, and this is why bread baking was usually part of a sacred ceremony dedicated to the Corn Goddess.
Sometimes the Goddess is shown with sheaves of corn in Her hands,
and Her worship would spread throughout the Western world in
both this and the Great Mother aspect. But She is also a Goddess of
Power, and this aspect would also spread.

Whereas the Dravidians had two deities who were so close they
were seen as two sides of the same being, and their multiple aspects
were understood to be only different representations of the All, modern mainstream religionists (people of Judaic, Christian, and Islamic faiths) continue to refer to this system as polytheistic. It is more
accurately monotheistic, though, because even Shiva and Shakti are
recognized as one Being—Ardhanari ("androgyne," from the Greek
andro—"man," and gyne—"woman"). Shiva Ardhanari is depicted
in sculpture as divided down the center, from head to toe, exactly
half male (right side) and half female (left side). The Dravidic structure can be seen in Neo-Paganism today with the usual divisions of
the modern Wiccan altar setting (as the Practitioner faces it) placing
the Goddess on the left, the God on the right, and both at the center.

This classic androgyne, or hermaphrodite (named for the two
Greek deities, Hermes and Aphrodite) was seen as evident in living
human form in anyone who possessed both sexual organs or was
homosexual in lifestyle. The gay male and gay female, so often condemned as immoral by mainstream religions, were once accepted
and honored as living representations of the God of Grace and the
Goddess of Power. Danielou further shows that, traditionally,
shamanic power has been associated with bisexuality, and that the
people giving divination in ancient times were garbed as hermaphrodites, with men dressed as women (as became traditional with
Catholic priests) and women attired with a phallus attached to the
girdle or otherwise strapped on.

Both dual sexuality and non-sexuality were seen as avenues to
spirituality and contact with the Divine, and thus in the worship of
Rhea and Attis in Greece, and Ishtar in Mesopotamia, as described
by Durant, men would castrate themselves and offer their sexual

organs at the altars. Aristophanes described the first humans as androgynous and, reflecting the Aryan influence, claims that these people were split into two sexes in order to keep them from becoming like the Gods. This same image exists in Genesis when the female aspect of Adam is removed from him to make a separate being (the word "rib" was substituted for the more accurate "side" in later Bible translations, and thus most modern Bibles have lost this significant connection). The original Adam then, described as being in the image of God, was an androgyne appearing as the Androgyne God. From the Hindu perspective, the ultimate goal of the human species is to evolve toward bisexuality, not away from it as is taught in the Judaic-Christian-Islamic systems. The aim of evolution, according to the Hindu view, is the reuniting of the sexes. There are animal forms in existence that have this characteristic (barnacles and some tree snails are examples) and the Tantric practices are directed to this same unity and equality in humanity, for if all people are both male and female, there can be no sexual dominance.

By 5,000 B.C.E., some 2,000 years before the Sumerian civilization got underway in the Near East, the Dravidians had come up with a mythology addressing the creation of the world in seven days, and devised names for the seven days of the week. They had a Tree of Life, revered the bull and snakes as sacred to the God and the Goddess as symbols of strength, life, and wisdom, believed that salvation came through knowledge and understanding (rather than by faith or good works), had ritual bathing, and practiced baptism— and indeed, there are scholars who believe that the Jesus of Christianity may well have been a student of Buddhism and Hinduism in His early years. Danielou believes an Orphic initiation may have been more likely, but others consider a trip to India to study religion (which was done by many philosophers of Greece and Rome) a more likely case. Buddhism, which began about the same time the Old Testament was being written, resulted from the Aryan attempt to restore Vedic orthodoxy to Hinduism, but it still contained Dravidic practices. The effort failed in India, with Buddhism being considered a heresy of Hinduism.

Nancy Wilson Ross, in her work, *Three Ways of Asian Wisdom*, writes that the ancient people of Sind developed mathematics; invented the zero; created algebra, astronomy, and geometry; measured the land and divided the year; mapped the stars and knew the courses of planets and the Sun; studied animal and plant life, knew the Earth revolved around the Sun, and did not think in terms of linear time as Western people have, but instead accepted the concept of an expanding and contracting universe in which the Life Force alternates between a period of dreaming (expansion) and resting (contraction to a singularity)—an idea that did not take hold in Western thought until 1965 C.E. They had developed the concepts of light years and the equivalent of modern astronomy's "island universes," yet very little consideration is given in Western textbooks to India as the cradle of civilization, and the mathematical skills ascribed to the Arabs were in reality simply what was transferred from India into Europe by way of Moslem invasions, caravans, and contacts with the writings of Alberuni, a Muslim traveler who wrote much about his visit to India 1017–1030 C.E. In this way, the Indian decimal system and math symbols came to the West, where they were known as "Arabic numerals." The Dravidians had calculated that the next dissolution of the universe began on what would today be written as 3102 B.C.E., so perhaps the Aryan invasions were anticipated as symptomatic of the beginning of the end.

The people of the Indus had a medical science, wove cotton into cloth, had a pictographic script of around 270 characters, which is still untranslated but seems to be similar to that used until recent times by the natives of Easter Island, and had ink for writing, perhaps on cloth "paper" (as is still done in China and Japan). Their tools were sophisticated, with such things as saws with teeth that allowed the dust to leave the cut, and they were exceptional wood carvers. The dead were buried in cemeteries of barrows, in stone circles with an urn or cistern built of stone slabs with a hole on the northern or eastern side, until after the Aryan invasions when cremation became the general method of disposing of the dead.

The Aryan religion was one involving fire sacrifices and altars, but the Dravidic aspects of ritual water use; reverence of trees, serpents, and bulls; veneration of stone pillars honoring the Linga (phallus) of Shiva; and ring stones honoring the Yoni (vagina) of Devi (another name for Shakti) as the symbols of divine creativity and the reproductive energies of nature, and the dualistic understanding of creation and destruction as the natural rhythm of the universe, were incorporated into what then became the new religion, Hinduism. Originally, the Aryans were scornful of the Dravidian deities and religious concepts, yet they were not only unable to eliminate worship of Shiva and Shakti, but the two deities endured and have become prominent in modern Hinduism. The Aryan patriarchal system was not successful in subordinating the position of women in Indian society until after the Moslem invasions, but in Southern India and in Punjab, where modern-day populations are strongly Dravidic, matriarchies are still the norm.

By the time the earliest civilization in the Near East began, circa 3600 B.C.E., at Sumer, the people of Sind were engaged in trade, and Hawkes concludes that one of the major exports was the Dravidic religion. The Sumerians bought many items from the Dravidians, but they had nothing to exchange, thus creating probably the first trade imbalance in history. The Sumerians also followed the clothing style of the Dravidians. The men of the Indus wore trimmed beards with no mustache, tied their long hair in a bun, and wore lightweight robes that left the right shoulder bare. The women dressed in short skirts with decorative belts at the hips, and wore numerous necklaces and large headdresses. Indus merchants had shops in the Sumerian communities and then in the Babylonian cities that followed in 2169 B.C.E., and it was not until the Aryan invaders began to take over Mohenjo-daro that trade disappeared from the region.

The Old Kingdom of Egypt began around 3500 B.C.E. and lasted until 2631 B.C.E. Mohenjo-daro is known to have been a thriving urban center with foreign trade and shipping bringing vast wealth into Sind from 2900 to 1700 B.C.E., and there was still no evidence of temples or organized clergy in Sind even when the first pyramid was being built in Egypt in 2780 B.C.E. In Egypt, the Old Kingdom came and went, the Middle Kingdom rose in 2375 B.C.E., a few years before the Sumerian Empire was destroyed by the Aryan tribe called Elamites, in 2357 B.C.E. It was about 2150 B.C.E. that the Aryans began to show up in the outlaying areas of Sind, and a few years later Hammurabi became ruler of Babylon, from 2123 to 2081 B.C.E., and created his code of laws based on the code of laws of the Sumerians. Indeed, the religion of Babylon was based on that of Sumeria, and the Sumerian language was the language of the Babylonian Holy Scripture, much like Latin was for early Christians.

By 1925 B.C.E. the Aryan tribe of Hittites conquered Babylon, and in 1860 B.C.E. Stonehenge was under construction in England, while civilization was beginning to appear in Palestine around 1800 B.C.E. At this time, Egypt's Middle Kingdom period came to an end, but the Indus civilization continued to prosper. The times are important, for they show that Aryan invaders were moving into the Near East and Indus regions; and the Dravidic population, rather than be governed, fled in all directions in a series of migration waves. They may well have been the first refugees of history, for they left their mark everywhere they went.

The Egyptian Empire period went from 1580 to 1100 B.C.E., and the literature of this time contains the fictional stories that would much later be incorporated into the Hebrew and Christian Bible and assigned to what would come to be interpreted by contemporary religious groups as actual historical people and events, like Solomon, Lazarus, and the feeding of a multitude with a few fish and loaves of bread. In 1500 B.C.E. a poem was written in Syria that would become the prototype for the Hebrew Daniel nearly a thousand years later, and by 1400 B.C.E. the Aryans lost control of their greatest secret—the forging of iron—and the Iron Age began for the rest of human society. By 1250–1200 B.C.E., the Aryans had finally succeeded in capturing and destroying the great cities of the Indus, and it is during this time frame, from 1200 to 700 B.C.E., that the Etruscans appeared in Italy to establish their great civilization with the same method of city-states as seen in the Indus.

Although in the past historians have generally agreed that no one knows for certain what were the origins of the Etruscans, except to say there is some evidence that they were Lydians who migrated from Turkey, it is increasingly seen as likely that these people were Indus refugees who fled Sind at some point during the early Aryan conquests, dwelled in what is now Turkey for a time, then moved westward into Italy when the Aryans swept into the region. The traditions of the Etruscans were not the norm for the Greeks or the Romans, and the equality of the sexes, casual sexual attitudes, lack of inhibitions, and a theology with smiling deities strongly indicate an Indus tradition.

The time of 1276 to 1200 B.C.E. was one of great Aryan activity. Assyria was unified in 1276 B.C.E., and the Mycenean culture disappeared in the Mediterranean, allowing for the rise of the Israelites under the rule of the Levites in Canaan by 1232 B.C.E. The rest of the Western world was active in warfare and expansion with Troy falling to the Greeks in 1193 B.C.E. The Aryan conquests were completed by now, the people incorporated into the societies they had overpowered, and their influence felt in the art, literature, and religion of their new subjects. Phoenicia and Syria entered into a Golden Age from 1000 to 600 B.C.E., and during this same time, the Hindu Vedas, Brahmanas, and Upanishads were completed, detailing the mythologies of the Hindu deities and setting the rules for orthodox worship that left the power in the hands of the Aryan Brahmin ruling class. The Assyrian Empire flourished from 732 to 609 B.C.E., Gautama Buddha lived eighty years from 624 to 544 B.C.E., and finally, after all this time and all these events, the first five books of the Bible, the Pentateuch, were begun in 621 B.C.E. The Roman Republic was founded in 509 B.C.E., after a series of wars against the Etruscans, whom they subdued and whose culture they attempted to obliterate (with some success), but from whom they gained invaluable information and techniques of civilization.

The Assyrian Empire ended in 609 B.C.E., a century before the founding of the Roman Republic, and the Babylonians again were the main power in the Near East until the rise of Persia. In 559

B.C.E., Persia entered its Empire stage, conquering Babylon in 539 B.C.E., Egypt in 525 B.C.E., and India in 518 B.C.E. It was under the rulership of these Aryan Persians that the Temple of Jerusalem was built. It was called the Second Temple because Bible mythology had stated that Solomon had built an earlier one, even though it was not at all in evidence. In fact, the one thing missing from history outside the Bible is the Kingdom of Israel. Meanwhile, Alexander the Great invaded India in 329 B.C.E., but only stayed four years before leaving with a Hindu yogi as his tutor in 325 B.C.E. By 138 B.C.E., genuine Jewish history began to be written by the Maccabees, but their writings are generally left out of the Bible of Christianity as unimportant. Prior to this time, Jerusalem was under the control of the Assyrians, the Babylonians, and the Persians, and the whole of the Kingdom of Israel consisted of the city and the outlying lands surrounding it.

The rest of Indus history and of its neighbors is fairly well known. The New Testament Gospels were written between 300 and 400 C.E. and the Roman Empire fell in 476 C.E.—this traditional date comes from the last great sacking of Rome (there were several such raids) by the Germanic tribes, who were, incidentally, Christians. Coincidentally, also by 400 C.E. the Great Goddess had been elevated into Hindu Vedic orthodoxy and the Tantric system was underway. India was invaded by the Huns from 455 to 500 C.E., then Sind was conquered by the Arabs in 712 C.E. The Moslem invaders pressed on throughout India from 999 to 1026 C.E., looting and destroying everything they felt offended their religion. They killed hundreds of thousands of Hindus from time to time, simply because they existed and their religion was considered an affront to the Moslem concept of deity. It was during the Moslem atrocities that the religion of Shiva and Shakti experienced an upsurge in popularity and the worship of the two deities began to flourish throughout South India and Kashmir, and spread into Indonesia in the wake of Moslem zealotry. Buddhism all but vanished in India by 1100 C.E., and from 1100 to 1610 C.E., Shiva was portrayed in heroic terms.

India was invaded by the Turks in 1186 C.E., and by 1236 C.E. the Moslems controlled extensive portions of India. Marco Polo visited India from 1288 to 1293 C.E., and Vasco da Gama arrived in 1498 C.E. to give Portugal a claim for a trading port, established in 1510 C.E. at Goa. After all these invasions, the wealth and grandeur of India was still legendary. The French and English fought a war in India over claims for trading rights from 1756 to 1763 C.E. The English won, and in 1765 C.E. Robert Clive was made Governor of Bengal. The British Crown took over control of India from the British East India Company in 1858 C.E., and in 1947 C.E., after numerous massacres of Hindus, defacing of Pagan temple art deemed offensive, and general mismanagement, the Crown granted independence to a nation they first divided into Moslem Pakistan and Hindu India, so that even today, the historic roots of India and Hinduism are in the territory of a fundamentalist Islamic State. Moslem East Pakistan was nearly destroyed by invading West Pakistan, but India intervened, and East Pakistan declared its independence from West Pakistan, changed its name to Bangladesh, and the "West" was dropped from the larger nation.

It was after India was opened for trade to the West that Dr. John Dee (1527–1608), who was court astrologer to Queen Elizabeth I (1558–1603), developed the Enochian system of ceremonial magic between 1570 and 1580 C.E. Already, the Jewish kabbalah had worked its way from Spain into the rest of Europe to become incorporated into the ceremonial system in Europe, under the tradition of Agrippa (1486–1535) and Paracelsus (1493–1541). In 1877 C.E. the Hermetic Order of the Golden Dawn was founded, and from 1875 to 1947 C.E. Aleister Crowley was a leading ceremonialist. In 1897 C.E. Charles Leland wrote his book about Italian witchcraft, *Aradia*, and in 1939 C.E. Gerald Gardner was initiated into Witchcraft. These are not isolated events, and in the next few chapters, the importance of these connections will become clear.

AUM and UMA: The Foundation of Pagan and Non-Pagan Religion

T he idea of Deity as dualistic had entered into human consciousness by at least 28,000 B.C.E. and formed the basis of metaphysical thought. People honored a "Great He/She" deity and held in awe and reverence natural-born hermaphrodites as visible expressions of the Deity, while homosexuality was understood and accepted as a manifestation of the dual aspect of Deity in human terms. The Indus civilization has been shown to be the first to emerge in the world, and the He/She deity found expression there in the union of AUM and UMA, commonly known today as Shiva and Shakti. These latter two names come down to modern peoples from the time of the Aryan conquest and the later Vedic writings of 1000 B.C.E. referring to events of 1500 B.C.E., so that while those names were definitely used around 1000 B.C.E., it is possible, but not certain, that they go back to the beginning of the Indus Civilization.

Klaus Klostermaier determined that the current Dravidic peoples of India are the descendants of the original inhabitants of Sind who fled to the south of India during the Aryan invasions, taking their beliefs with them. They have basically preserved the emphasis of the Great Goddess and Her Consort in their version of Hinduism, and have reverence for the names Shiva and Shakti, which implies that these are indeed the names of the Sind deities. The link between Hinduism and the God and Goddess of Sind has been noted also by Jacquetta Hawkes, and by Will Durant in his immensely readable *Story of Civilization: Part I, Our Oriental Heritage*. Yet, for these writers, the focus is primarily on Hinduism, rather than on the Sind religion that predates and was incorporated into Vedic Hinduism.

Of the two aspects of Deity, it was the female that received many different names to express Her various attributes, but the male retained His name and had the attributes listed afterward. There is Shiva Nataraja (Shiva, Lord of the Dance), Shiva Ardhanari (Shiva, Half Male and Half Female—or Androgyne), Shiva Digambara (Shiva, Sky-Clad—or Clothed in Space), Shiva Pasupati (Shiva, Lord of the Animals—or Lord of the Beasts), Shiva Linga (Shiva, Phallic—or Creator/Fertility God), and Shiva Mahayogi (Shiva, Great Teacher or Great Ascetic), to name just a few of the 1,000 listed names of Shiva.

The Goddess, however, became known by specific names. Shakti is "Power," Devi or Mahadevi is "Goddess" or "Great Goddess" and is the the Supreme Being, Durga ("Inaccessible") is a War Goddess, Anapurna is the "Bestower of Much Food," Jaganmatri is the "Divine Mother," Parvati is the "Earth Mother," and Kali is the "Black Mother" (an aspect of Devi who represents the dark side of Nature, for all life passes through death to enter into new life, and Kali is that passage). This, too, is only a partial listing of the numerous names for the Goddess—yet all the names belong to one Deity.

It is the name UMA that clearly demonstrates how this religion of the Indus was spread throughout the Near East. UMA is the name of the Dravidic Great Mother who rules humans, animals, and plants; is considered a liberator through spiritual transcendence; and later came to be associated with the lion and a mountain (perhaps due to the influence of early Aryan invaders as they moved across Sind and the Near East). This name is popular in the Southern region of India and the Punjab, areas of Dravidic concentration.

UMA Parvati

UMA became the Sumerian Goddess Uma, whose father was named Sin (a literal interpretation of Her origin, for She did in fact "come from Sind"). She then became the primal Goddess of the Babylonians who adapted their religion to such an extent as to retain the Sumerian language for their sacred scriptures. As some historians believe it likely that the Sumerians were early settlers from Sind, the connection between the Mesopotamian religions and that of the Indus Valley is even more obvious.

The Horned God, Lord of the Animals, is traditionally matched with the Lady of the Mountain. Shiva and Parvati are seen in Crete as Zagreus and Cybele, as well as throughout the Near East under various names. Their symbols, the bull and snake, the phallus and vagina, and in some areas, the tiger and lion, are prevalent from the Neolithic Age onward. The emblems of the Aryan deities who came after the Dual Deity related not to nature and animistic or pantheistic views, but to natural phenomena such as lightning, fire, and rain, and to a personification of what were considered human virtues, such as honor, sharing of goods, etc. Whereas the oldest religion of humanity was based on nature and humanity's place therein, the Aryan religion was centered on man as apart from his natural surroundings, with the Gods being called upon for security and success in dominating others. Nature was something to be propitiated through sacrifice, rather than to be celebrated as part of the unity of humanity and the universe.

Danielou, who spent many years in India and became an initiate in a Shivan sect, wrote that Shiva was also called Ann in prehistoric India. This name was sometimes shared with the Goddess, and can be traced through the Hittite Ann, Canaanite Anat, and the Celtic Ana, but also is seen in the Sumerian Anu. Ann has become Saint Anne in Brittany, and the name appears as the mother of the Virgin Mary. This quality of Shiva to be sometimes identified as female most likely relates to the Ardhanari aspect. But perhaps, from the Christian point of view, the most surprising name applied to Shiva is Isha ("Lord"), which is the Aramaic pronunciation for

Shiva Ardhanari

the name recognized today as Jesus. While this connection between Shiva and Christ will be covered later, one should be reminded that Christian tradition also recognizes that there were many names applied to their object of devotion, including Joshua.

The deities of Sind will be referred to as Shiva and Shakti for the most part, but one must keep in mind that aspects of either, especially the Goddess, have come to be proper names. This does not reflect a multitude of Goddesses or Gods, but one Goddess and one God, co-joined and approachable in different ways, for different purposes, under different names depicting various aspects. The duality of the God and the Goddess is a monotheistic religion that recognizes the inherent oneness in nature that results from a natural twosome—a whole has two halves, yet remains a whole, and the whole may be divided into numerous segments (aspects), yet remain a whole. Ardhanari is All, yet Shiva and Shakti. The Tantric definition of AUM, which is collectively the sound of the name of God pronounced to include all vowels, gives meaning to each letter—A is Grace and is male, U is Power and is female, M is the All and is both male and female in union. The letters of UMA have the same definition, but it is the U that comes first to express the Goddess of Power, then as M in union with Her Consort, A, the God of Grace. Either emphasis is acceptable, it depends on one's needs and preferences. To contemplate the Two as One, one focuses on the M, Shiva Ardhanari. This system of using letters to represent a being or attribute of deity was passed along to the religious traditions of other peoples through Dravidian contacts, migrations, and later Aryan conquests.

Trimurti
(Brahma-Vishna-Shiva)

The mythic patterns of the God and the Goddess spread from the Indus with the symbols of each intact. The concept of Trinity, for example, was derived from both deities. Shiva had the trident, and is still portrayed as

Three-faced (Shiva Tri-murti, with "murti" refer-ring to form or embodi-ment) and in this "Three-in-One" aspect can be found the source of mod-ern Christian belief. Holger Kersten in his work (focus-ing on the similarity be-tween Hinduism and Christianity) sees the Christian Trinity as derived from the Vedic, with God the Father as Brahma, Vishnu as God the Son (that aspect of Deity which becomes incarnate from time to time), and Shiva as the Holy Spirit, the ele-ment of Divinity that makes all the rest possible and which in the Judeo-Christian tradition is not to be blasphemed. One may curse in God's name or

A Christian Trinity.
In different parts of Europe may be seen fig-ures similar to the above, wherein three faces are united in one head.

that of His Son, but *never* by the Holy Spirit. Thus is the reverence of Shiva preserved today in the West.

Siva is also called Three-Eyed (capable of destroying or creat-ing) and this relates again to His position as the source of the three aspects of the Trinity, but it is Shakti who is more frequently mani-fested in terms of Trinity. As Devi, She is the Mother of the Universe who divided Herself into three Mother Goddess forms, Sarasvati, Lakshmi, and Parvati. She is also Maiden, Mother, and Crone as Sati, Parvati, and Kali. There are a number of female Trinities that have come down to Western Civilization, including the Three Fates (Lachesis, Clotho, and Atroppos), the Morrigu (Ana, Badb, and Macha), the Norns (Triple Moon Goddesses Urd, Berdthandi, and Skuld), and the Triple Earth Goddesses (Persephone, Demeter, and Hecate). The latter held a dual position of Earth and Moon, which was not uncommon for a goddess who could represent both the Earth and the magic power used to direct the Earth's energies as the Moon directs the Earth's tides. The original female Trinities entered into the later Aryanized religions of India and the Near East, and resulted in a conflict between Goddess worshippers and Aryan conquerors.

In the purest form of the Aryan religion, the only thing that could be remotely considered a Trinity involved three male deities—the Father God, the Lawgiver, and the Warrior. In Vedic Hinduism, these were initially Brahma, the Creator; Vishnu, the Preserver; and Indra, the Great Warrior. Then, as the religion merged with the Dravidic, Indra was deposed by Shiva, as the Destroyer. As early as 1915, however, scholars (such as W. R. Elmore) were writing about the incorporation of Dravidic deities into modern Hinduism. In the Northern European Pagan system, the Gods were Odin, King of the Gods; Tyr, the Lawgiver; and Thor, the Great Warrior. No Aryan Goddesses of Power were recognized in India (in keeping with the European tradition) until the Dravidic Goddess began to infiltrate Aryan Hinduism at the side of Her Consort, Dravidic Shiva.

For centuries, the elevation of the Goddess in the Dravidic strongholds of India was considered a heresy. Between 700 and 1000 C.E., worship of Shiva predominated in India. Subsequently, Klostermaier chronicles numerous religious purges in various regions of India depending upon which emphasis the ruler followed. Followers of Vishnu slaughtered those of Shiva, and when the Shivaites came into power (particularly from the fourteenth thru seventeenth centuries C.E.), the slaughters were reversed. The few females that had been deified by the Vedic Aryans were generally presented as dutiful mates to the Gods, tending to domestic chores, just as in Europe. But the Aryans did have an earlier tradition—from the days before their expansions—when the Mother Goddess was honored. To have returned to this glorification of the female aspect of Deity would have weakened the position of power and elitism that had evolved among the leaders and warriors in Aryan society, and so Her worship in the conquered lands had to be eliminated. This is the background that led to the diminishing of the Goddess in favor of the God in the Near East religions. It was a practice echoed by the Northern tribes of Goths, Teutons, Germans, Anglo-Saxons, and Gauls in Europe.

The Vedic Hindus were Aryans who worshipped the sacrificial altar (the Vedi) and emphasized the importance of fire and the ritual maintenance of a fire in each home. These same elements are typical of all Aryan tribes, and involve complicated and detailed instructions for the carrying out of religious duties. These duties were the responsibility of a designated, hereditary priesthood who received exorbitant gratuities from the people they ruled in exchange for their services as intermediaries to the Godhead. Their elite status was enumerated in law, and maintained by required separation and restrictions in marriages to those of their own class. They traditionally had contempt for images and temples (coming from a mobile background), but in India the blending of the Dravidic and Vedic traditions, along with the opportunity to become a more settled people, led to the creation of a religious form that overrode these admonitions to become modern Hinduism. It was this accession to images and temples that the Aryan tribe named Levites initially sought to eliminate in their theological control over the Hebrews.

The God and the Goddess of the Indus were represented by the Sun and the Moon interchangeably. This was acceptable because They are One, and it depended upon which aspect was being considered as to whether the Sun or Moon served as the best emblem. Generally, though, the Sun and the Moon designate the God and the Goddess respectively. Vedic Shiva is typically depicted as wearing the Crescent Moon in His hair, but this may have come from the Aryan influence, showing the Moon Goddess as a smaller part of the male deity. Shiva is described in Hinduism as being like a million suns, so as the Sun God, He brought Parvati into Hinduism as part of Him. Fertility, the seasonal changes of solstices and equinoxes, the phases of the Moon, and the schedules for planting and harvesting all became part of the cycle of life that was the basis for the first religion in Sind. Nothing has changed—not since the original idea from at least 28,000 B.C.E. The names of the deities may be altered, the reasons for the observances redefined, but it is still the same whether the Winter Solstice (as an example) is the Wiccan celebration of Yule, the Christian celebration of Christmas, or the Jewish Festival of Lights (Chanukah or Hanukkah)—it is the return of the Sun that is celebrated. This applies to most of the other religious holidays of today.

From the Aryan point of view, the worship of a Phallic God was disgusting. They failed at first glance to recognize that there was a greater concept involved than mere penis worship, one that encompassed the veneration of the creative forces. The male element as Linga could be represented by anything from a standing stone to a tree stump, and was the symbol of the creative energy that dances in each and every living thing in the form of dynamic molecules. The female element as Yoni, generally represented by a ring stone or one with a depression or a cleft, gave expression to that energy in the shape of the life produced. The whole concept was not vulgar, and most modern Hindus would be at a loss to understand why anyone would deem it so today. Although Hindus with Western contacts have experienced this reaction to the Linga, and some have expressed consternation at their religion being considered primitive, they also wonder why Westerners would label their beliefs in this way while flaunting in jewelry, art, and worship a brutally executed man as a popular image of God.

The Linga depicts an understanding of the workings of Nature and the Earth on a cosmic and microscopic scale. The Dravidians were not ignorant—they had sciences that are only now being rediscovered, after centuries of burial under restrictions imposed by religious rulers. Shiva's dance is the motion of cosmic energy, just as it is now known that the molecules in everything that appears to be solid are actually in a state of constant excitement.

Shiva in the Shape of the Linga
God of Fecundity

Shakti, through the Yoni, defines the form of these dancing molecules—be it a tree, a rock, or a person—and thus everything that
contains this energy is alive in one way or another, even "living
rock." Today science knows that these molecules are being traded
off with those of other objects; that there is a constant interaction
between molecular structures, which makes the concept of pantheism all the more rational.

**Yin Yang
Creation Principle**

The concept of the Linga and
Yoni are seen in the Chinese Yin and
Yang, evidence that the religion of
Sind traveled there as well. The ithyphallic Horned God, sometimes seated in a Yoga position on a low throne
or stool, has been found across Europe
from 6000 B.C.E. At times the deity is
depicted as a bull, a bull with a human
face, or a phallus with a human face.
There are ancient burials at Lepenski
Vir in Yugoslavia near the Danube
that are made in the yoga position.
Danielou believes that the religion spread to Southeast Asia and is
reflected in the religions of Cambodia, Java, and Bali. The images of
the Linga and Yoni are thus directly connected to the first civilizations and beliefs of humanity, radiating outward both East and West
from the Indus Valley.

From the Dravidian expression, the Linga is the source of the
energy, while the Yoni determines what that energy creates, for the
Goddess takes that energy into Her womb and gives birth to all
things. For this reason, She is called Power. It was in order to detract
from the Goddess that the concept of "matter" being evil arose in
the Aryan-based belief system and cosmologies. The pre-Vedic system saw that energy and matter were interrelated—God and Goddess in union—and that matter was not evil, but the form the God
took in substance. To label matter as evil would be to label God's
creation as evil, and that would make God unworthy of devotion.

This problem has tormented the Judeo-Christian theologians for 2,500 years, and the only purpose such negation of substance serves is to authorize the subservience of women and perpetuate the persistent view of inequality.

The Vedic Hinduism of today is an orthodoxy, begun in 1000 B.C.E. and continuing through 500 B.C.E., that blends Aryan and Dravidic traditions. Until that time, the two systems functioned as rival denominational factions, with the latter being considered inferior by the ruling Brahmins, and with many regulations of the Aryan tradition being imposed upon the Dravidic. The progression of Shiva mythology—myths that cover the same themes over and over but with slight variations—shows a gradual improvement in the status of the Dravidic God, with subsequent improvement for His Consort, Shakti. This has resulted in an "Aryanization" of Shiva/Shakti, as evidenced by the Puranas, written instructions for the worship of Shiva, dating from between 900 and 1100 C.E. There has also been a "Dravidization" of Aryanism, as is apparent from the alterations in accepted Vedic mythology. One must expect that change over several thousand years is inevitable.

The original religion of Sind, while not the same as Hinduism, can nevertheless be found in the religions influenced first by the original Dravidic faith, and then by the Aryan distillation that followed, and migrated with the Aryans from the entire Sind region. Hinduism also has many denominations, but unless that denomination is Tantric (dedicated to the study of universal power, Shakti, and its expression) or Shivaism (often spelled Saivism, and dedicated to the God Shiva), it has a pronounced Aryan basis. The sects dedicated to Shiva and Shakti simply have less Aryanism than Hinduism in general, but the influence is still there.

Wendy O'Flaherty, in her work, *Siva, the Erotic Ascetic*, categorizes the overlaying of myths by several primary themes that are reorganized over time with different results by various religious schools of thought. In one case Shiva is ordered by Brahma to create the world, but He takes so long in preparations that the job is turned over to Vishnu, a clear slam at Shiva's creative powers. Yet, in a later myth, the same story has a different twist—the reason Shiva's preparations were taking so long was because He was going to make humans perfect and immortal, but Brahma was afraid of competition from humans and wanted to be worshipped, so Vishnu was given the task, and carried it out so that humans were mortal and had bodies susceptible to any number of frailties. The result of this myth is to elevate Shiva as a selfless God who wanted a perfect creation, but Brahma becomes selfish and cruel in His need for worshippers. Vishnu comes across as either a shoddy workman or a toady for Brahma in the revised myth. Indeed, a subsequent myth has Shiva so annoyed at how Brahma has messed up creation that He condemns Brahma to have no worshippers. Today there is only one small and neglected temple in India dedicated to Brahma.

One can see the interplay between Aryan and Dravidic elements in these myths. Each side tries to elevate its own deity while negating the other's. So Shiva curses Brahma, and naturally, the follow-up myth by the Aryan faction has Brahma curse Shiva so His Linga falls off—terminating the creative symbol of Shiva. But then, the next version states, Shiva, being called the Unperturbed, only allowed that to happen because it gave Him a chance to show His power by restoring the Linga. And on it goes until at last, in one myth, Brahma and Vishnu both worship the Linga of Shiva.

As the mythology improved the status of Shiva, and therefore, Shakti (especially as Parvati and Devi), there was a reaction from the Brahmin caste against the Dravidic incursions into the Aryan faith. The initial intent of the conquering Aryans was to establish their dominance over the large population they ruled through precise and complex religious rituals that invalidated the religion of their new subjects. The deities were mocked in mythology and degraded in terms of what they represented. Parvati was described as being ridiculed by Shiva for Her dark skin, and She then had to practice Yoga to acquire a golden color that pleased Her husband. Shiva was described as a lord of vampires, terror, and thievery; one who haunted the burning places (Aryans cremated their dead and imposed this practice on the Dravidians) covered in ashes. He was a beggar and a seducer of women, unfaithful to His wife, and yet too intent on Yogic practice to create the world when ordered to do so by Brahma.

The association of Shiva with the Aryan god Rudra is one that has continued to confuse people learning about Hinduism and Shiva. Janet and Stewart Farrar in their book, *The Witches' God*, report the terrible aspects of Shiva and label Him as a pre-Aryan god who evolved from what is considered a more primitive deity, Rudra. Klostermaier, however, calls Rudra an early Vedic deity. The train of events appears to have been that the Aryan tribes had tribal gods, and Rudra ("Reddish") was one such god. The qualities of Rudra were assigned to the Dravidic Shiva, so that by the time the Vedas were being written, the two had been incorporated into one god. Yet Shiva is described, not as red, but as white or silvery. To see Shiva as evolving from Rudra is to miss who Shiva is. Shiva predates the Aryans and their deities; Rudra is an Aryan deity of comparatively more recent lineage.

Although depreciated in mythology, the fact that the myths were passed on to the people of Sind caused the myths to never end in the way they were begun. Somehow, Shiva and Parvati always managed to turn things around to their favor in the storyline, and the unpleasant aspects given to them simply did not have the intended impact. Although Shiva failed to bring about creation, the myth was revised to say it was because He could only create immortal beings, and Brahma demanded mortal humans to worship Him. The God of Grace has not been diminished, but shown to be more loving. The Vedic Brahma, however, deliberately makes humans suffer.

Shiva and Shakti have continued to be shown as deities of compassion, love, and understanding. It was as though They smiled with tolerance upon Their enemies until at last, Shiva the Unperturbed and Shakti the Great Mother overpowered the Aryans with kindness. This is not to say that there were not some sects that developed from the Aryanization of the Two as demonic—there were indeed blood sacrifices and assassin sects born from the initial meddling of the Aryans. It is because of this that modern Hinduism has different denominations of Shivaism and Shaktism, and some of these are banned because of their brutality. Only modern religious freedom in India has allowed the widespread resurgence of the original Sind form of the God of Love and Goddess of Power to be identified with a positiveness unimpeded by Brahmin rhetoric.

The advent of Buddhism (624–544 B.C.E.) is the most recent concentrated attempt to remove Shiva and Shakti from the Aryan faith of India. The Aryan deities of supremacy have always been secular and political. They had come into being much later than the Lord and Lady of the lowest level of the European Aryan religion, and had reflected the needs of a specific class of people—rulers and warriors—who did not exist in the previously communal organization of the tribes. By the time Mohenjo-daro fell in 1200 B.C.E., the

Worship of Buddhist High Priest

Aryans had a completely organized system that relegated the Dual Deity of their earlier times into lesser deities permitted for the masses, but not significant enough to ensure a pleasant afterlife. The priestly rulers held all the power to communicate with the gods of consequence, so while the fertility deities could still be honored by the ordinary people, they had to address the male triad of superior gods (through the designated priesthood) for matters of importance, like life after death. These deities were created for the political purpose of sanctioning the power of the rulers and the warriors who supported them.

The Buddhist reform movement sought to purge Hinduism of its Dravidic elements and coincides with the reformational writings of the Pentateuch occurring at nearly the same time. Buddhism is today considered a heresy of Hinduism, which is why there are not many Buddhists in India and why there is warfare between Buddhists and Hindu Tamils (ardent Shivaites with an ethnic Dravidic background) in Sri Lanka. The earlier shunning of Shiva and Shakti did not prevent the people from slowly elevating their native deities within the imposed worship system, and, today, Shiva is seen as the One Alone—having successfully moved from the role of ridiculed outsider to that of Supreme Deity. He is considered the One in Whom resides all aspects of matter and being, and in Whom the Universe dissolves and appears in many forms. But Buddha (and other Brahmins like him) was dissatisfied with the inclusion of Dravidic influences in whatever form because this undermined the position of the priesthood. Buddhism, too, developed new forms, but even with the return of Sind elements in the practice of Tantric Buddhism, the role of the female is diminished in accordance with the Aryan tradition.

The Vedic mythologies, meant to uphold the power of the rulers and the warriors, had progressed to the point where Brahma was minimized and Shiva glorified. Vishnu also came to a secondary place as the devotee of Shiva. This is illustrated in the myth about Brahma and Vishnu arguing over which of Them was supreme, when a fiery pillar appeared before Them. To investigate this phenomenon, Vishnu traveled downward as a boar and Brahma traveled upward as a swan, but neither found the end of the pillar in either direction. They met again and Vishnu admitted His failure, but Brahma lied, claiming He had found the other end and was therefore the Universal Lord. At that point, the column of fire opened and out stepped Shiva, the Infinite, praising Vishnu for His truthfulness and placing Vishnu as second to Himself, and reprimanding Brahma for His lie and condemning Him to remain without worship from then on. This tradition was carried over to early Christianity when cathedrals and churches were named, not after God, but after members of the Holy Family and saints.

Buddha restated Hinduism with an emphasis on the caste system, multiple forms of sexual discrimination against women, domination of women by men, alienation of women from religious participation except as subservient to men, and the superiority of the ruler and warrior caste over everyone else. All of these elements are absent in devotion to Shiva, but can be found in Buddhist societies, such as Japan with its Samurai tradition and low status for women. The later development of a Tantric Buddhism is considered a heresy, as it attempts to bridge the Aryan and Sind ideals. The concept of any power being in the female, however, was unthinkable in the original Buddhism.

The Brahmin religious rituals were secrets handed down from fathers to sons, and the sons were required to carefully learn the proper procedures for each ritual, lest anything be done wrong and ruin the ceremony. If the words were garbled or stumbled over; if one thing was done out of proper sequence, the entire ritual was ruined, no matter how far along it had progressed, and it would have to be started over from the beginning. These ceremonies could be very costly and time-consuming as they were, but to repeat them could be more than the participant could afford or handle. The very fate of the souls of the dead depended on the ceremony for cremation, with the preliminary rites, and later benedictions being done exactly right, or the departed would suffer the consequences. The same adherence to detail has been passed along into the methodol-

Brahmins at Their Devotions

ogy of kabbalistic rituals in ceremonial magic, and the celebration of the Catholic mass and other sacraments.

Buddhism was all but exterminated in India, with many Buddhist priests being tortured to death or consigned to vats of boiling oil, and Hinduism was able to continue its development toward an even more Dravidic acceptance and emphasis. The denomination of the "Heroic Shiva" (the self-realized adept sees the whole body as the expression of various aspects of the Divine) arose between 1100 and 1400 C.E., and took on a program of economic and social reform that included the abolition of caste and sutee (the burning of living widows on the funeral pyres of their dead husbands), and a return to the Sind practice of burial of their dead. A strong missionary movement was launched (just when Europe began to experience its first "Renaissance" in the twelfth century) by this Lingayat denomination (so-called because its adherents wear a Linga symbol around their necks—much as Christians wear a cross), and its impact is still being felt today.

The Lingayats could have originated as an attempt to return to a purer Dravidic faith—just as the Brahmins had tried to restore the Aryan elements of faith in Hinduism through Buddhism—but the

Heroic sect gained power in various regions, and became the state religion in the province of Mysore in 1498 C.E. Denominational warfare existed in various parts of India as the followers of Vishnu and those of Shiva disputed over which deity was Supreme. The mythology became convoluted, and the success of either God in the same myth depended clearly on where it was being presented. If the region was dominated by ethnic Dravidians, the greater was Shiva; if the region was dominated by the ethnic Aryans, the greater was Vishnu. Yet the Shivaite principle of freedom of worship has been officially accepted in modern India, although the actual practice is always a point of dispute—as it is in America.

The presence of AUM and UMA can be traced through the religions that came after them because their influence has been strong and enduring. The changes made in the basic naturalistic religion of Sind make a fascinating study as the ebb and flow of societies have taken the basic concepts and reshaped and redefined them to suit the needs of the worshippers. The politicalization of religion was an Aryan innovation that required the invention of virtually secular deities, and from that has come the heritage of the religious wars that have plagued humankind for thousands of years. The time is right for this to end; for matters of conscience and the soul to be one of personal decision, not one to be determined by state dictates or church intimidations. To comprehend the power of the religion of the God and the Goddess and its subsequent influence on modern religions, it is necessary to consider how the Aryans reacted to this faith when they encountered it in regions other than India.

The Aryans and Sind

When the Western religious experience is viewed as a whole, it becomes apparent that there are two basic patterns of belief at work. At one time, at the earliest level, there was only one pattern—that of the Dual Deity. This system evolved naturally and reflected the environment of nature and the place humanity held within it. From the beginnings, just as is indicated in the Biblical book of Genesis, humans were one with the world in which they lived. It was a sort of paradise, not because everything was perfect, but because humans knew who they were and how they fit into the scheme of things. This was a triumph of human metaphysics. It was also the religion of a communal society and the religion of Sind.

Not until the formation of a ruling and warrior class did the concept of deity change. For this reason, the Father God/Lawgiver and Great Warrior God are not a natural, but a political, development that reflected the need to legitimize the change in society from communal to hierarchical. Aryan society was reorganized to meet the challenges of population growth and subsequent territorial expansion. Leaders were supported by their warriors, and, in time, the society became segmented between those who fought and those who tilled the earth, tended the flocks, and created the goods necessary for living. Initially, women and men were equally mobile in Aryan society, with farmers and women capable of bearing arms for the ruler, but over time laws were created that stifled this and tied some members of society to the land, others to service, and others to males. The reason the laws moved in this direction was to distance the practice of worshipping the political deities from that of worshipping the natural deities. All segments of society initially practiced the same religion (Alain Danielou shows that the yogic burial position was used in Yugoslavia as early as 6500 B.C.E.), but with the advent of a political system, theology became politicized. Those who were not in the top segments of the political structure of rulers and warriors did not have ready access to the deities of these classes. As the power of the upper classes increased, so did the powers of their gods, until, at last, the Dual Deity became a lesser form of religion in Aryan society, and the ordinary people could only approach the greater gods through their emissaries, the warrior priests and the god-king.

The priesthood that came into being was magic-oriented, as the priests administered the sacred duties insuring the obligation of obedience from the common people to their rulers. Since the God and the Goddess were obvious in Nature, it was necessary to create a cause for which people would have to turn to another set of deities, and from this need came the concept of salvation. This meant that the Dual Deity was no longer enough for human religious expression and was pushed aside in Aryan theology. During the conquests of other lands still practicing the original form of worship, the Aryans named the local religions as anathema (cursed, damned, and evil) and worked hard to excise the older deities from popular veneration. The power of the priesthood depended upon the power of the rulers and warriors, and they were all members of the same class. This has become expressed in modern India as caste, while in Europe the clergy generally came from the nobility, as the Church was considered a good place to put extra sons who could not look forward to a legacy nor do well enough in battle to support the King at arms. There were variations, with some members being inferior to the nobility (friars), others similar (bishops and archbishops), and some superior (cardinals), even to the secular ruler (the pope).

In Europe, the original religion was relegated to a position of tolerated lesser faith—a country faith of superstition and old practices, rather than an elevated level of religion typical of the higher strata of society. In India the Aryan faith became infiltrated by the religion of Sind. This happened because the conquered Dravidians were not part of the Aryan society, did not function and grow with that class system, and were the original inhabitants of the land wherein the ancient religion of the God and the Goddess had evolved. By the time the Aryans arrived in the Indus Valley, Shiva and Shakti were the living and socially entrenched deities of the Dravidians. By remaining in the Indus, the Aryans became more settled and found their religion changing to adapt to the land and its people. But the Aryan tribes did not stop in India; they moved on into Asia Minor and the Near East, taking the lessons learned from the Indus experience with them.

This is where the great divergence takes place, then. It did not happen in Europe, where country faith and noble faith, the natural religion and the political religion, had a livable arrangement of tolerance, nor in India where the ancient beliefs held fast and merged with the Aryan faith over time, to the point of re-establishing the Dual Deity as Supreme, but it occurred in the Near East. This becomes the heritage of modern Western religion, the battle between pure Aryanism (which did not even exist as divorced from the earlier system in the homeland of Aryan theology) and the religion of Sind spread throughout the Near East. From this conflict evolved the Judaic, Christian, and Islamic faiths. Their basis is not Near Eastern, but a branch of Northern European, devoid of the naturally evolved Deities, and based solely on the secularly created gods of the nobility.

To achieve a pure Aryan religion with the God of the Brahmins, the Aryans had to repudiate and denounce the practices that had undermined their system in the Indus Valley. It is not a coincidence that, as Kersten points out, Moses comes from the Sanskrit word Manu, "Lawgiver," and that this name is the root for Mises, Manes, and Minos. These names are not individuals but positions of authority in the Aryan societies. That the Judaic tradition is descended from Abraham—a Brahmin, as Merlin Stone shows in her work, *When God Was A Woman*—should come as no surprise. Nor is it a coincidence that the timing of the historical beginnings of the Israelites (1232 B.C.E.) is soon after the fall of the Mycenean Kingdoms (1250 B.C.E.). When one looks at the larger picture rather than focusing only on the Near East and Mediterranean, it becomes clear that after the continued invasions of the Indus (from 2150 to 1200 B.C.E. when the last Indus City fell to the Aryans), the events of the Near East were triggered by the sudden collapse of this last line of resistance. Warriors were free to spill into the Near East at a tremendous rate, and by 884 B.C.E. the Assyrian Empire was their new stronghold. Merlin Stone details the movement of the Aryan tribe of Luvites across Anatolia into the land of Canaan. There, in accordance with the archaelogical evidence as reported by Neil Asher Silberman, they encountered the Canaanite refugees from the fall of the Mycenean Kingdoms—"Israelite" nomads who made calf artifacts of worship, revered snakes, and had re-established themselves on hilltops after deserting their cities in the valley. The Luvites became the Levite rulers of the Hebrews, and two centuries later, the Aryan Buddhist reform movement began in India, during which time Jewish colonists were known to be living in Egypt, where a missionary site of the Buddhists was located in Alexandria.

The succession of historical events involved great activity from the Aryan people, including the rise of the Persian Empire, whose people are today's Iranians and acknowledged by historians and anthropologists to be an Aryan-speaking race. The building of the Temple in Jerusalem was actually constructed under the rule of the Persians in 520 B.C.E., and fits in perfectly with the need to promote the Aryan faith and dismantle that of the God and the Goddess of Sind. The Temple was a concession to the needs of the Israelites being ruled by Aryan Levites. The Levites themselves were separate from the other Israelites, were forbidden to intermarry with them, received the first fruits of all harvests, had property rights that amounted to fiefdoms, and were by law the only ones permitted extravagant dress and displays of wealth. These are the same regulations that applied to the Brahmins of India, to keep them segregated from, and in power over, the Dravidians they had conquered.

The myths and symbols of the deities of Sind had come into the Near East and lay at the foundation of Near Eastern religion from the time of Uma of the Sumerians in 3600 B.C.E. The earliest Bible stories of the Old Testament can be traced to those of Sind circa 5000 B.C.E., with the Sumerians, Babylonians, Egyptians, and Syrians further building upon this tradition the stories that are erroneously believed by many people today to be of Hebrew origin. The story of the Creation in seven days came from Sind 7000 years ago. The 1920s Egyptologist James H. Breasted and Will Durant trace the tale of the seven years of plenty and seven years of famine as coming from Egypt in 2980 B.C.E.—two centuries before the first pyramid was built.

The basis for the Ten Commandments can be found in the nearly word-for-word transcription of the Sumerian law codes created between 2474 and 2398 B.C.E. Hammurabi took these Sumerian laws and adopted them for Babylon during his rule from 2123 to 2081 B.C.E. Moses as Lawgiver came from the Assyrian Mises. And from the Egyptian literature of 1580-1100 B.C.E. comes the prototype of Solomon, the story of Lazarus, and the feeding of the multitude. These various non-Hebrew myths were borrowed and re-stated as the Word of God by the early Aryan writers of the Old Testament beginning in 621 B.C.E. But to understand what the Old Testament is about, and therefore the basis of modern Western religions, one must look to the purpose of its being written and the identity of the enemy of the Aryan God.

One of the emblems of Shiva and Shakti that was incorporated into the religion of the Sumerians, and then carried forward through time among the religions adapted from the Sumerians, is the Tree of Life and Knowledge. The tree imagery has been brought into the present time by the book of Genesis and the story of the Garden of Eden. The Tree was supposed to be located in the midst of the Garden, which may imply the center of belief rather than mere placement—hence, in the midst of the Sind religion in Kashmir, the first region of the great subcontinent encountered by invading Aryans. The Dravidians believed that knowledge was to be valued and was the source of immortality, and they represented their God and Goddess as trees. If one knew the interconnection of all life in energy, one would understand that humans were naturally immortal and that death was only a passage from one form of life to another—no salvation was needed for there was nothing evil in the functions of life. This concept lies behind the term "Original Sin(d)"—not being ashamed of being human and alive—the original religion of Sind.

**Symbol of
Wisdom and Learning**

The Indus people cherished learning and enjoyed a life free from guilt and from a priesthood. Wisdom became associated with Sind early on, and being called a thing of "sin," was denounced by the noncivilized Aryan warrior-priesthood whose power depended on their control of the people they ruled through the requirement of fire sacrifices to appease God. In fact, just about anything from Sind was recognized as such, and thus the term for something non-Aryan was Sind, or sin. Kersten, in *Jesus Lived In India*, shows the etymology for the word sin as derived from the German "die Sintflut" ("Great Flood"), and Sint came from the High German word meaning "great flood." This became "Sundflut," or the flood of sin, which Kersten sees as connected with the Aryan contact with Sind, from which India receives its name. Durant explains that the name Sind, derived from the native word, *sindh* ("river"), was translated as "Hindu" by the Persians, and then "India" by the Greeks. Today, except for Sind in modern Pakistan, the progression is no longer readily apparent. Klostermaier also states that Sind is the Sanskrit for "river," and further recounts that modern Indians still see their land as stretching from Sindhu to Sindhu, meaning from the Indus River to the Bay of Bengal. Kersten points out that the region known as Sind today, in the southern portion of the Indus Valley, is subject to frequent flooding; and, indeed, newspapers described flooding that killed over 100,000 people as recently as in the autumn of 1992. The German and the Indian come together through the Aryan Levites' reporting not about events in Mesopotamia, but in Sind.

Locating Eden

In Hindu tradition, it was at the source of a Kashmiri river Sind, near the Cave of Amarnath, that Shiva let Uma Parvati in on the secret of creation. Thus, the very crime of Eve—seeking knowledge (and thereby immortality) from the beautiful god who is always depicted draped in snakes of wisdom—was originally a gift from the God of Sind to His Goddess. This is Energy explaining to Matter how it all works. One must keep in mind that Hinduism is a combination of Aryan Vedic and Dravidic Sind, and thus to the Levites what is accepted in this amalgamation of mythology in India was seen as an impurity to be denounced by true Aryans, and something to avoid in Canaan.

The Serpent of Eden is therefore another image from Sind, and may indicate, as Stone suggests, the earliest known use of snakes as a means of attaining an altered state of consciousness for the purpose of shamanic divination and expanded awareness. Snakes were associated with the Dual Deity, but particularly with the Goddess, and it seems that women were the first to use them for prophecy. It is known today that if a per-

**Specimen of Ancient Persian Breastpin
The serpent was the respected symbol of Wisdom.**

son has received small doses of venom to build up immunity, the venom from certain snake bites will produce the effects noted in classical writings describing oracles. Stone recounts the events that occurred when a man who worked at a lab in Florida collecting snake venom for medication was bitten accidentally and later talked about the sensations that overwhelmed him. His hearing became acutely sharp, he heard sounds like that of many birds chattering (and birds are associated with the Goddess and prophecy—to become in modern times the quip, "a little bird told me"), and he had visions. For him the experience was intense and profound. This man was not a Pagan, but for a short time, he crossed over to an ancient Pagan practice and described it in terms unaffected by religious influence or restrictions.

The idea of a Holy Land predates the Judaic application and comes from the Dravidic (and later Vedic Hindu) religion, being the land that extends from Sind to Sind, as previously noted. As Klostermaier reports, Hindu beliefs imply that one cannot be really considered a Hindu until one has visited the Holy Land—India. In some areas, certain stones, trees, hills, and mountains are centers for pilgrimages, which is a custom adopted into Judaism, Christianity, and Islam. Kersten shows that the Holy Land of the Judaic tradition was actually centered around Kashmir, site of the earliest Aryan conquests in India, and Klostermaier's study of Hinduism tells of Hindu mystics who have traditionally described Shiva as "milk and honey," and "the bright light" (he is usually described as having silver or white skin, but is sometimes portrayed as sky blue, or white with a blue throat caused by His drinking a poison that threatened to destroy the human species), and by 621 B.C.E., when the Aryan Levites began writing the Pentateuch, they named for their own possession the "land of milk and honey." In a sense this was true, as the Aryans did rule the Indus Valley, the land of Shiva; just as Eden, or Paradise, was not located in Mesopotamia's Valley of the Tigris-Euphrates, but in the Valley of the Indus and its main tributaries.

The descriptions of Eden in the typical published Bible are not clear, and so interpretations have been added that relate rivers and

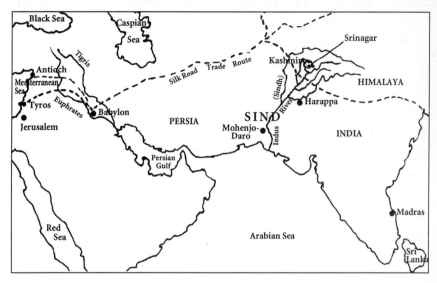

Kashmir—The Holy Land

locales to familiar areas around Mesopotamia. These names do not accurately relate to the text, however, and did not at the time of the original translations. Since the translators were working from the assumption of the Holy Land being in the Near East, they related everything in the Bible to that region. The main river of Eden, with its four branches flowing out of the garden, however, is more reasonably the Indus. In Genesis, the land of Havilah "where there is gold," through which the main river of Eden flows, is a reference that definitely fits the irrigated farmlands and the legendary wealth of the Indus Valley, and one of its great cities, Harrapa, whose name is evocative of the strange name used in the Bible. India's rivers provide 90 per cent of the total gold production of India today, so that just as when Genesis was written, there are rivers of gold. When one considers the theory of consonantal shift, called Grimm's Law (1819), with the softening of the consonants over time and the systematic changes in words moving from one language to another, the development of Havilah from Harrapa is easy to see. The river that flows from Eden and supposedly encompasses Ethiopia (which in reality has the White Nile on one side and the Red Sea on the other, and is not "encompassed" by either) is more likely to have bordered Kashmir, so that what is called Cush in the Bible is Kush, the passes of which were used by the Aryans to enter Kashmir.

Simply looking at a map and considering geographical features is sufficient for locating Eden, but Kersten traveled there in preparation for his study on the connection between Jesus and India. He details the place names that are in the Bible, but located in India. The Indus, called Sind in Kashmir (for Sind simply means "river"), has along its route all the places of Bible fame, and even the tomb of the Lawgiver known as Moses. Kersten, however, writes from the perspective of rationalizing Judeo-Christian religious beliefs and does not go back far enough in time to see the entire picture. His focus was on the sources for the Bible stories as events rather than on the origins of religion, and so he does not make the connections between Sind, the Dravidians, Hinduism, and the development of Judaism.

Kersten makes a convincing case for the Kashmiri origins of Judaic beliefs, but that is only part of the picture. The Aryan invaders of the Indus Valley began in the northern regions and in the western fringes of Sind around 2150 B.C.E. and portions of the northern area fell to their control long before the southern region. This is why the "Judaic" tradition of Canaan did not get started until after the final big push of 1250 B.C.E. had seen the destruction of Mohenjo-daro and the fall of the Mycenean Empire. Naturally the stories of the Bible would relate to Kashmir as that was the first stronghold of the Aryans—that was "home" for centuries to the Aryans before entering Canaan, but it was also the older home of the Dravidians and their deities.

With this perspective, then, when the Bible describes the rivers of Eden, it is immediately apparent that while there are four distinct branches that pour into the Indus from the north of the valley, the Tigris-Euphrates has no connection with the rivers around Ethiopia, nor are there four large rivers connected to these two anywhere in Mesopotamia—nothing fills the description of the Garden of Eden and its rivers so clearly as does Sind with the Indus River, four large tributaries, a history of immense wealth, a religion of trees and snakes, and historic origins of civilization.

Kersten shows that the names of Biblical places are easily found in India, and relate to one another as the Bible describes them—Mount Pisga, Beth-peor, Heshbon, Moab, and Nebo are places in Kashmir named Pishga, Behat-poor (today called Bandipur), Hasbal, Moab, and Mount Nebo, the latter of which overlooks Bandipur and the Kashmiri highlands. By following the directions given in the Bible and using a map of Kashmir, Kersten traveled to the sites and located the tomb of the Aryan lawgiver, Moses, which is enshrined and identified in Kashmir as such. What happened in Palestine, then, is very much like what happened when America was settled by Europeans.

With the "New World," the names of the "Old World" European towns were transported to the new colonies. Just as there are places in America named for sites in England, France, Spain, Holland, Sweden, Norway, and Germany, so there are places in the Near East named for sites in Kashmir and the Indus Valley. And just as one would be hard put to apply historical references of the European places to those bearing the same name in America, the problem is likewise encountered in the Near East to make Bible descriptions fit the places in Palestine. With all the "holy" sites in the Judaic Holy Land, the warning is given that these are merely the "traditionally" accepted locations. In some cases, there are duplicate sites, as for example, which mountain in Palestine is supposed to be Mount Sinai (where Moses was supposed to have gotten the Ten Commandments), although now the connection with Sind and Kersten's further investigations into Kashmir bring the site out of Palestine and back to Sind. When one considers that the "ai" ending is Greek plural, the source of the Ten Commandments reverts to "Sin"; Sind, Babylon, and then carried into Assyria via the Indus colony of 3600 B.C.E., Sumeria.

By listing numerous examples of words that are identical in spelling and meaning from Kashmiri and Hebrew, Kersten agrees with historian Abdul Ahad Azad that Kashmiri is derived from

Hebrew. Yet it is more likely to be the other way around in the sense of real time. The Hebrew words are derived from the Kashmiri. The Kashmiri Hebrews of Kersten's study were Aryans who came to Kashmir, moved onward to Mesopotamia, with some of them then returning (the so-called "Lost Tribes"). The indigenous Dravidians were either absorbed into the culture of the remaining Aryan ruling population (having altered the Aryan faith to become Hinduism), isolated into their own cultural niche, or emigrated to other lands in the face of Aryan invasion.

The Biblical concept of God, and, later, the Son of God, being the Good Shepherd with His devotees called His flock, was adopted from the earlier description of Shiva as the Divine Shepherd with His flock of followers. He is also the reconciliation of opposites, and forms the Balance between Creation and Destruction—the natural realities of the Universe, the Earth, and all life. This idea of balancing opposites has always posed a problem for the Judaic interpretation of God. The Judaic deity is supposed to be a God of Grace and Love, but also of Wrath (all of which are qualities of Vedic Shiva), but Judaism has difficulty explaining why a good deity would allow bad things to happen to His faithful followers.

The Book of Job is a case in point, wherein it is expressed that the good suffer, and must still give praise to the God that allows this to happen. With a total disregard for the individuals involved in this particular tale, Job is supposed to be pleased because, after his first family is destroyed by God, he receives a new family. Not much value is placed, then, on those who died. It is not the Biblical Satan who tests Job, but the very God Job is supposed to worship and turn to in his times of need. Throughout the Bible, it is God rather than Satan who wreaks pain and suffering on His children. This union of suffering with goodness then is what led to such extreme self-punishment as flagellation, pole sitting for years at a time, mortification of the flesh, and so forth by early Christians. It is still going on today in small Christian sects, and is reflected on a larger scale by the Fundamentalist Christian injunctions against any form of sensual pleasure.

Most of the early saints of Christianity were people who were otherwise comfortable in life, but were consumed by guilt for having a pleasant life. They engaged in self-mutilations and starvation fasts, exerted themselves to find new ways to demean their flesh through not bathing, covering themselves with dung, and committing other acts that would be offensive to the body and society. No wonder the average Pagan, as Tacitus wrote, found the early Christians to be bizarre and abhorrent cultists. The Dravidians, with their religion of the Dual Deity, did not see pain as evidence of one's goodness, nor did they consider a pleasant life to be a cause for guilt.

The Aryan dilemma arose because their negative Rudra aspects were added to Dravidic Shiva during the initial attempt at subverting His worship, and this was carried over into the subsequent attempts at purifying the Aryan beliefs. Prior to this, people were more pragmatic, accepting that bad things do happen through chance, or luck, or fate, but that people are also responsible for the consequences of their actions, either in the present life or the next, in the form of Karmic retribution or advancement. The problem with such a concept, of course, is that it removes the need for a magical and superior priesthood to intervene between God and the ordinary person. With the religion of Sind, there was no innate human guilt; but because the Judaic version of the religion of the Aryans exempted the Dual Deity, there was no innate human innocence, and when taken to Christian extremes as during the Middle Ages, should even a newborn baby die before baptism, entry into heaven was denied.

There are many points in the Pentateuch alone that show the connection with the earlier religions of Sind and Vedic Hinduism. The search for the origins of Western religion does not entail a need to prove the validity of religious writings. It is no more necessary to prove the reality of Vedic Krishna than it is to prove the existence of Biblical Moses. What one must keep in mind is that the Bible, like the Vedas, is mythology, and one cannot look upon Biblical people as historical personages and attempt to relate them to real time and events. Thus there are no pharaohs mentioned by name in relation to Moses, and there are no dates to align Biblical events in relation to historic events.

The statement by God to Moses, giving His name as "I am that I am," has long puzzled theologians, but is directly traceable to one of the Hindu names for the Supreme Being—Tat ("That")—which puts a whole new perspective on the meaning of this otherwise mystical phrase. The Prayer of Manasseh is one of the Apocrypha (books usually not found in Protestant Bibles, but located between the Old Testament and New Testament of Catholic Bibles), as are the only books of real Jewish history, Maccabees I and II, written in 138 B.C.E. Manasa, however, is the name of the Snake Goddess whose worship is still widespread in the Bengal portion of India. It was Shiva who first was called Beloved Father, Highest Truth, Grace, and Good Shepherd, and these titles were passed into the Bible by the Aryan Levites to describe their deity. Stone has shown that the very name of the Judaic God, Yahweh, is derived from the Sanskrit word for "everflowing," and she linked this to lava and the Aryan fire culture.

The Star of David is another symbol of Sind, and is actually the Dravidic Star, showing the dualistic union of Shiva, as the triangle, and Shakti, as the inverted triangle. In Hinduism, the two triangles are placed together to form a six-pointed star, and that star is placed in a circle to represent the Dual Deity in Time. It is no coincidence that this symbol appears in the Bible and is related to David, for David is Dravidic, and the stories about Saul, David, Bathsheba, Solomon, and the Queen of Sheba are a metaphorical retelling of the religious development of India as restructured by Aryan Levite reformists.

Saul is the name of a valuable and durable tree of India, and as a Tree, represents the Goddess Devi (turned into a male as was customary in the writing of the Bible—just as the Goddess Ashtoreth was made into the God/Demon Astaroth—to prevent any taint of a female deity of power being a rival to the Aryan God in an Aryan scripture). The name of Shakti as Devi ("Goddess"), was also given a sex change, to become the male Devil. The mythological progression recounted in the Old Testament shows that the Goddess Tree had been deposed by the God—Dravidic Shiva—in the Aryan Hindu blend of religion, so that He now assumed the position of Power. David's dancing before the Ark of the Covenant as it was carried into Jerusalem was frowned upon because this showed that Shiva, the Lord of the Dance, had literally entered Jerusalem in the form of His religion before the Aryan deity could be established.

David later weds Bathsheba ("Daughter of Shiva"), showing that the female aspect is under his domination, and they have a son named Solomon. It is Solomon who represents the final stage of integration of the Dravidic into the Aryan. The Shiva aspect of wisdom is defined through Solomon, who now becomes advisor to the mysterious Queen of Sheba. Her origins have been seriously debated for centuries, and she has been considered to have come from a variety of places, including Ethiopia and an area of the eastern coast of the Arabian Peninsula just across the water from the Indus Valley. It is not surprising that her homeland is a matter of dispute and confusion, for she is, literally, Shiva's Queen—Shakti—and the story is meant to prove the superiority of Aryan Judaism by receiving Shiva's wife as a petitioner to be counseled and sent to an obscure mortal king, to be his submissive and now-mortal wife. The entire story denotes the diminishment and final banishment of Shakti, and the absorption of Shiva as an Aryan. At least this was the purpose of the story, although not the reality of the situation.

Throughout the history of Judaism, the Levite priesthood had to contend with the rivalry of the religion of Sind, and there are numerous references in the Bible to the continued practicing of the Old Religion (such as the women weeping for Tammuz at the temple doors; and dressing up in their finery, as Gomer, the wife of Hosea did, to worship Ashtoreth with sexual unions at the Temple). The myths of Shiva and Parvati have been restated numerous times throughout the Western world, and were well known at the time of the writing of the Bible. It was because of the influence in Palestine of Minoan Zagreus and Cybele, Greek Venus and Adonis, Roman Cybele and Attis, Babylonian Ishtar and Tammuz, and Egyptian Isis and Osiris that the Aryan religion had to be codified and made orthodox. The Bible is not exactly history, but rather propaganda designed to obscure the older traditions that saw everything in the universe as part of and therefore accessible to the Divine, to promote the Aryan faith and to secure the power of the Levite priesthood that ruled the Hebrews.

Christianity and Sind

The modern Western languages have been traced back to the Indo-European roots of Sanskrit, yet history is taught without the recognition that modern religious concepts—like words—come from the early intermingling of Aryans and Dravidians in the Indus Valley. Western society retains the Near East as the source of civilization and falls short of the true beginnings in Sind, for humankind was indeed "born in Sind," as the Bible states. The mythology of the Bible serves as a pointer to the reality of the influence of the Indus deities in the Near East and the foundation of modern mainstream religions in AUM and UMA.

The Judaic religion is both a repudiation of the early Sind religion and an attempt to create a pure Aryan worship form based only on the God of the ruling class. The Aryan tribes that conquered the Near East were Medes, Persians, Vedics (Hindus), Hittites, Luvites (in Asia Minor) and their kinfolk, the Levites (in Canaan). It was this latter group that created the religious system and mythology in Canaan designed to ensure their power and destroy the God and the Goddess. Yet, even so, the tradition would not disappear—the rule of a political God might be enforced, but the elements that went into the formation of the natural Dual Deities were still in evidence, and still spoke to humanity in nature. Talmudic and popular Jewish tradition have related these elements to Yahweh as the Dual Deities Elohim and Jehovah. Again, God is venerated as male, but is described in terms of male and female aspects. The struggle continues to this day in Judaism, and the conflict has passed into Christianity.

It would doubtless come as a shock to some Christians to discover that Jehovah refers to the female aspect of God, and that by invoking God Jehovah, they are actually calling upon the Goddess. But then, most Christians do not understand the Bible in the same way as the Jews, which is probably why the vast majority of the Jews in Israel today are not orthodox, but are secular Jews. This literature does not truly belong to Western Europeans, and cannot be comprehended because the ethnic tradition is not there and has not been absorbed in order to be taught in a European context. The Jewish elements in European society were kept segregated for the most part, living in their own sectors of the otherwise local communities, in Jewish ghettos. These people were shunned, abhorred, and discriminated against as a matter of course in Christian Europe. The Jewish traditions that went into the makeup of the Bible were not incorporated into European culture, but the literature was, and those traditions were thus subject to misunderstanding. The Europeans essentially fought for centuries over an "alien" and nonrelevant theology, while all but annihilating their own native and ethnic theology of Wiccan Paganism.

The reason Catholicism retains so many followers—far and away vastly more popular than all the Protestant sects combined—is because the early Church brought in elements of the European Pagan tradition. These elements included the association of water, wells, and springs with purity and the Goddess, and with Pagan shrines rededicated to the Holy Virgin and other Goddesses who were designated as Christian saints (Saint Brigid, as an example). The time-honored traditions of Pagan holidays were retained by renaming them as Easter, Christmas, and so forth, while keeping the customs of each—such as Ostara egg exchanges, bunnies (the Hare of Pagan fertility), and the baking of phallic cakes (which Philip Rawson writes in *Primitive Erotic Art* was done in Italy, Germany, and France until recent times, and further, that "The Sacred Member," a large phallic image, was carried in the Easter procession near Naples until the eighteenth century C.E.)—in a Christian framework. The August harvest festival honoring Artemis (Goddess of the Moon) as virgin/mother, or Hecate (Goddess of the Dark of the Moon) as the Protectress and Teacher of the Secret Arts, became the feast of the Assumption of Mary into Heaven. The gift exchanges celebrating the rebirth of the God at Winter Solstice as a baby to be nurtured by the Mother Goddess have been retained under the guise of Christmas, altered for adoration of the Virgin Mary and Baby Jesus.

In the United States of America, the 1990 Census and a study by the Association of Statistics of American Religious Bodies show that of the 137 million church attending people of America (55 per cent of the total population), the Roman Catholic Church commands a following of nearly 53,500,000 people. This is more than all the Protestant sects combined (excluding three million Mormons, who are not "Christian" in the traditional sense). The very things that the Protestant groups detest in Christianity—veneration of the Mother of God, saints, "holy water," rosaries, and statuary believed to dispense miracles, to name but a few of the modern complaints—is what draws people to Catholicism. There are many who feel "at home" in the "Holy Mother Church" simply because they are feeling the cultural ties of their heritage. The one aspect that repels, however, is the demeaning position allotted to women in general, while revering the Virgin Mary.

While emphasis of the gentle aspects of the Goddess results in an Aryanized Mother of God, the powerful aspects have been eliminated. When the dual sexual attributes of the Divine are viewed from the female's perspective, the Goddess then becomes capable of war and violence—a Kali or Morrigu (also called Morrigan)—and yet the Goddess of love has often been equally a Goddess of war and aggression. The different sides of the Androgyne remind one of the different sides of Nature, but the Aryanization of the Goddess in Christianity results in the creation of half a person—the Eve seeking wisdom and immortality is denounced in favor of Mary, the obedient handmaiden. As Virgin Mary, the Goddess becomes the symbol of the perfect, dominated female with total submission to the Aryan Lawgiver Godform. This is another reason why the modern Pagan movement in America is so attractive to people of European descent. For them, it is like rediscovering their roots, without the detractions of the political deities, making Paganism more relevant and innate than the Catholicism that has absorbed the original Pagan elements.

The Scriptures of Christianity owe much to the early Greek Christian writers for their form and substance. Later translations from the Greek into Latin, and then into the common languages of the various nations, resulted in some literally correct words with mistaken meanings (a subject unto itself); as for example, the word "rejoice," which Durant points out in Greek usage actually meant "hello." It is also no coincidence that many of the attributes of Jesus are identical with those of the Greek resurrected god, Dionysus, whose religion continued until the fifth century C.E. and predates not only Jesus but also the Old Testament, by many centuries. Kersten recounts that Dionysus, like the later Moses of the Bible, also crossed the Red Sea dry-footed, had armies led by pillars of fire, had rays of light coming from his forehead (as typical of Moses), or (in another version) from his third eye (as typical of Shiva), and he descended a mountain with a code of laws inscribed on stone. That latter pattern can be traced to other pre-Judaic sources as well, such as King Minos of Crete descending with laws in stone from Mt. Dicta, Hammurabi of the Babylonians receiving his from the god Shamash, and Zoroaster of the Persians, 660–583 B.C.E., returning from the mountain of Ahura-Mazda with his laws in stone after God appeared to him amid thunder and lightning—a mere forty years before the writing of the first books of the Old Testament were begun.

Kersten gets caught up in the hunt and recounts in detail numerous similarities between Moses, Zoroaster, and Rama of the Rig Veda, but his approach is meant to prove the relationship between Jesus and India. If he went back further, he would have discovered the Sind and the Vedic conquerors, which would further show the Old Testament to be an irrelevant and extremely flawed relic of ancient mythology. Why, indeed, should one be encouraged to waste one's time with Moses when one can go to the source—Shiva and Shakti?

As with the Jewish Moses, the Christian myths of Jesus are those of Dionysus. The symbols of the miraculous birth, the baptism, entry into a holy city on an ass, the Last Supper as a sacrament, suffering, death, and resurrection are all from Dionysus, and may be traced back to India, from where, as Danielou reports, even the myths of Dionysus say he came. The first miracle of each involved turning water into wine; the Holy Communion also is seen with Dionysus. By the association of Dionysus with Shiva, and Jesus with Dionysus, the connection between Jesus and Isha is not difficult. Kersten claimed to have located the tomb of "Jesus" in the town of Srinagar in Kashmir, marked in the traditional way (a large stone carved to match the feet of the deceased) and that the marker indicated nail holes in the feet of the prophet from Palestine, Yuz Asaf. When one remembers that one of the names traditionally ascribed to Jesus is Joshua, the link to Yuz Asaf with the softness of Hindu pronunciations is clear.

Klostermaier refers to the efforts of Greeks and Romans to associate Hindu deities with their own pantheons, with Shiva equated to Dionysus, and some historians (like Danielou, and Kramrisch in her work, *The Presence of Siva*) make a case for a stronger connection between Dionysus and Shiva. Dionysus came into Greece from Thrace first as a fertility goddess, was then seen as the horned god fathered by Zeus with his daughter Persephone (there is a similar story in the Hindu mythology of incest between Brahma and his daughter, the Dawn), and developed over the centuries into the Son of God who dies to save mankind. His mythology is identified as relating to the crops, with mourning for his sacrificial death followed by celebrating his resurrection. This god was very popular in Greece and the Roman Empire, and his worship even included the forerunner to the traditional Easter Sunrise service, with the women going into the hills to greet the reborn god at dawn. The story of the suffering, death, and resurrection of Dionysus was ritually repeated, just as is that of Jesus in Christian churches at Easter, and his followers believed that they would never die because of him. The recitation of a litany and the acting out of roles in Christian churches is directly related to the older Greek religious practices.

As with the worship of Shiva, ecstasy was the form of worship and the name of the followers of Dionysus, *bacchoi* (bacchants with the ch as a "k" sound) is naturally similar to the Indian word for religious participants, *bhaktas.* It was the religion of Jesus that eventually deposed that of Dionysus in Greece, but then the similarities were sufficient to make the transition relatively painless. The groundwork for the early Christian belief in reincarnation (John Romer has presented an excellent study of the early pre-orthodox beliefs of Christianity in his television film series, *Testament*) was laid with the image of Dionysus as the seed reborn to a life of happiness.

Durant associates Zeus with the sky-god of the Vedic Hindus, but allows that Dionysus (like Shiva) was a more primitive deity who was only later accepted onto Mount Olympus, just as Shiva was accepted into the Vedic Trinity after displacing the Vedic God Indra. Interestingly enough, in the first two centuries of Christianity, there was occurring in India a resurgence of Shiva missionary work, during which time the Greek philosopher Apollonius of Tyana visited India to study. The missionaries of India were also very active in Greece and Rome, as evidenced by references in Tertullian's *Apologia versus gentes* in 197 C.E. (written in defense of Christianity), and the Indians were an integral part of the Roman economy. The trade between Rome and India was a thriving one, for India supplied the Empire with various manufactured goods, from textiles to wood and metalwork, to animals for the games.

Because the contacts were so well established, it should come as little surprise that the New Testament Gospel of John begins the lineage of Jesus with, "In the beginning was the Word, and the Word was with God, and the Word was God," for this is a reflection of the

Indian Goddess Parvati, whose name is derived from the words for "Earth" and "The Word." What John describes as the beginning is the time of the ancient Mother Goddess with Her Consort, who is with Her, and as Ardhanari, is Her. She, then, is "The Word brought to Earth," or "made Flesh," and thus does the Jesus of religion become the representative of both the Goddess and the Androgyne combination of the Dual Deity. The problem with the New Testament, of which this is but one example, is that the people who wrote the various books and constructed the Christian theology did not have as firm a grip on the meanings behind the theology of Judaism as did the early Levites, and were furthermore influenced by the known Greek and Hindu religions of their times. They took the symbols and threw them together in a manner that has had Christian theologians arguing over their intent ever since. Millions of people have died in religious wars during the nearly 2,000 years of Christianity because of disagreements over the interpretation of the incongruous passages culled from revised and discarded sources. As Danielou, Durant, Romer, and others point out, this new religion only became important when Constantine used it for the imperial unification of Rome and as an instrument of power.

The mantra for Shiva—"Aum namah Shivaye" or "Shivaye namah"—means "God's name is Shiva" or "Shiva is the Name" [of God], and the use of this mantra motif was used in the Jewish cry to honor only one God, and is further evident in the Islamic mantra, "There is only one God and His name is Allah", although in this case it is redundant since Al-Lah means "the God." The innovation of Islam is the removal of any proper noun that can be associated with God. In other words, since all the names of God relate to the Dual Deity, God has no name but "God"—which is a more accurate translation of the Arabic. There is, however, the suppressed but nevertheless existent sexual opposite of Allah in Al-Lat, "the Goddess," who was worshipped before the start of Islam. These names can be seen as an inheritance from the Egyptian Asar and Aset (Osiris and Isis in the Greek language). In the very structure of language, the female aspect cannot be denied any more than one can realistically

Morning Prayer in the Desert

state there is "right," but only "right." The existence of this word implies its opposite, be it "wrong" or "left." There is no neutral, genderless word for God, but there is Ardhanari for both genders. What is significant about this development in the Near East is that the Levites who ruled Canaan were nevertheless a product of the diluted Aryanism of India. So while they were attempting to establish only one political deity as God, they nevertheless used the terminology of Hinduism, so that the very first Commandment amounts to a recitation of the Shiva mantra.

The ultimate goal for the worshipper of Shiva is to achieve that level of knowledge which makes it no longer necessary to practice rituals or duties, meditate or proclaim the faith in any way, for the body itself is the temple of God, and life is the ritual therein. Instead, one may act as a child or as though insane because of ecstasy, with outbursts of singing, dancing, and wild abandonment. These actions are all considered to be signs of having reached the knowledge of truth; the Self experiences the Universe as identical, connected. The belief is that Shiva does not require ritual, but allows it for the benefit of the less enlightened. His love for people allows Him to let them display their love for Him—it is a mutual obligation born of love, much like a mother loves her child's messy Valentine card because it is the expression of love for her from her child. Shiva simply *Is*, and it is expected that all who love Shiva will love all beings as part of Him. This theme, too, is an aspect of Christianity that has been expressed in the ecstasy of saints (like Theresa of Avila in Spain) and the theology of various denominations (such as the Shakers and "Holy Rollers" of Colonial America, and the Pentecostals of today).

Shiva is described as having stretched out the Earth and as dwelling in all places and objects. He is in the stones, plants, and animals of the Earth; the Master and Lord of all creatures and the Universe. It is believed that He grants favors, dwells in the hearts of good people, and appears in a form because He loves people and wants to free them from continuing rebirth into the world due to Karma. He is called the Great Physician, the Killer of Death, and the Victor Over Death. All these attributes might well sound strangely familiar—they are themes borrowed and placed in the Old and New Testaments of the Bible. Just as the idea of freedom through study, ritual, austerity, and virtue has been incorporated in the Judaic and Christian system through an emphasis on religious education, service to God through good works, and membership in a religious community, the theme of salvation from sorrow coming from both one's own efforts and the grace of Shiva is echoed in the injunction that one is saved by the grace of God, and good works are the proof of this.

Shiva was denounced in the Aryan texts of the Brahmins for being the deity of the humble, and for teaching the lower castes the mysteries of religious practices, just as Jesus was denounced by the Pharisees in the Christian texts. In India, a separate priest class of the worker caste has maintained in relative obscurity the distinctive rites of Shivan worship, without the influence of Aryan Brahmins. They have been part of the undercurrent of pre-Aryan practices in India for nearly 4,000 years, but in Europe, the massacres of nonconformists have resulted in the near disappearance of Pagans or Wiccans throughout the centuries of Christian domination. That anything survived to the present time is indicative of the power of those beliefs and traditions.

The concept of rebirth is also in the New Testament, and initially emphasized the physical rebirth of reincarnation. This was only deleted from the Holy Writings some 500 years after the Crucifixion, at the Second Council of Constantinople in 553 C.E., and at the insistence of the Byzantine Emperor Justinian and his wife, Theodora (who had a habit of having her opponents murdered). Kersten has written from the point of view that Jesus was an Essene, and that he had studied Buddhism and Hinduism during travels to the Holy Land—Kashmir—during the "missing years" of his life story, and that he was known and has been chronicled in India under the name of Yus Asaf.

The actuality of Jesus, his travels, his crucifixion, and his manner of surviving this torment (with great attention to the details of the Biblical accounts related to Indian techniques, and Indian literature that refers to Jesus and his activities in India prior to and subsequent to his crucifixion) are all matters that Kersten has made into a lifetime study. He brings into English print details and proofs from Indian sources that shed a whole new light on the Bible stories, and help explain why the Jews were so annoyed with the deification of Jesus by the Christians, and why the early critics of Christianity considered it a religion of the ignorant. The prospect of Jesus being involved with Hinduism and Buddhism came long before Kersten, however, and Jesus was recognized as a Vedantist by Pundit Shunker Nath in *Christ: Who and What He Was*, written in two parts in 1927 and 1928. But beyond understanding who Jesus was and what his history was, lies the meaning and source of his teachings.

Christianity is therefore based not only upon the Aryanism of the Levites, but also upon the amalgated beliefs of Sind through Greek and Roman contacts. Kersten points out the numerous similarities in the birth and life stories of the Hindu deity Krishna and Jesus as the Christ. At one time, there were Chrestins in Asia Minor (Helena Petrovna Blavatsky, who wrote *Isis Unveiled* and founded the Theosophical Society in 1875, used the term "Christna"), and it was only after they had been destroyed as heretics by Papal command that all followers of Jesus were called Christians. The Greek

The Minotaur of India

word chrestos meant "anointed with oil," while Krishna, which is commonly pronounced as Krishto in India, refers to one who attracts everything and is thus is the personification of God. In Hinduism, this is an incarnation of Vishnu, whose own name refers to the energy and light of the sun, and thus He is formless until incarnated. Nevertheless, in the story of Krishna, this incarnation of Vishnu is a devotee of Shiva, which is reasonable when one remembers that Shiva can be interpreted as being representative of the Holy Spirit. In Christian tradition, one may escape retribution when one curses in the name of God, or His Son, or the Virgin, but one must never speak in blasphemy against the Holy Spirit. Peter Abelard barely escaped being condemned as a heretic in twelfth century France when he dared to name his school after the Holy Spirit, calling it the Paraclete ("The Comforter").

The incorporation, then, of Shivan ideals into Christianity is really not surprising since the name Christ is the Aramaic form of the name Krishna, and indicates that it is very likely that the historical person now known as Jesus was engaged in missionary work for Krishna, and in the minds of the early followers in Europe, he became inextricably associated with the God He was preaching about. All the themes and mythological patterns of Krishna (which predate Jesus by as much as 500 years), from the Star of the East to the Wise Men and so forth, have been assigned rightly to "Christ," but wrongly to "Jesus." Krishna, as an incarnation of the Aryan God of Creation, Vishnu, was a lifelong devotee of Shiva. Klostermaier recounts Krishna's initiation into Shivaism as described in the Mahabharata. This story is then used in the Mahabharata to explain why Krishna and Shiva are the same, since Krishna is supposed to be an incarnation of Vishnu; the Hari ("Yellowish-green One") Krishna and the Hara ("One Who Takes Away") Shiva are One in the same sense that God and the Son of God are One. Shiva is considered to be All, and is the God, while Vishnu is an aspect of Shiva that is manifested from time to time through incarnations, and is therefore God's Son. The "Hari" refers then to those incarnations upon the Earth through the Earth Mother (Uma Parvati).

With Christianity, Christ is born of the Earth Mother (Mary/Parvati) as the Son of the Heavenly Father (Father God/Shiva as All), but the preacher, Jesus, was assimilated as the deity Christ (Krishna)—which is why the people of Nazareth who are said to have known Jesus in his youth, and his human family, did not consider him a deity. The recognition of the difference between Jesus and Christ has been noted by numerous historians and writers, most recently by A. N. Wilson (*Jesus: A Life,* 1992), but previously by Ernest Renan, Albert Schweitzer, Francois Mauriac, Geza Vermes, Joseph Campbell, John Romer, James Breasted, and Arnold Toynbee. Modern theological discussions at seminaries debate the "meaning" of Jesus and Christian teachings, and many religious writers continue to view themselves as good Christians while reinterpreting the Bible as metaphor. When one adds to this that Shiva's name Isha is pronounced as Jesus in the Aramaic, the mythology comes full circle.

There is one other consideration that should be noted here, and that is the dating used for Krishna. Kersten, writing from the religious point of view, shows the Vedas as dating to around 4,500 B.C.E., the Indus Civilization as existing at 2,500 B.C.E., the Aryan "Lost Tribes of Israel" settling in Kashmir during the 6th century B.C.E., and the missionaries sent out by Emperor Ashoka of India to the Near East and the Mediterranean around 250 B.C.E. The Vedic tradition of pushing back time to give validity to their theology is just as active in India as in Palestine. At the alleged time of a "historic" Krishna, the Indus Valley had not yet seen its first Aryan. It is known that the Aryans did not arrive at the outer reaches of the Indus Civilization until 2150 B.C.E., and since the actual texts written about Krishna did not come into existence until 1000–500 B.C.E. the timing is obviously inaccurate, but deliberate. In this same way, the Levites made the history of the world begin at a time when in reality, there were other thriving civilizations. If anything, this can be seen as an Aryan tradition that further binds the Levites to the Vedics of India. It is this deliberate confusion of time in religious texts that make them unreliable for history. One may just as easily use *Bulfinch's Mythology* for a study of Hellenistic history as the Bible for Judean history, or the Vedas for Indian history. Unfortunately, Western society is so accustomed to accepting the Bible as literal truth that historians still get tripped up and mingle the real with the mythical, even after acknowledging that the Bible is not historically accurate.

While Shiva is revered as a "personal God" (a usage later adopted by Christian theologians who had access to Indian theological works for centuries before the orthodoxy of the New Testament was decided), the "personal" aspect of Dravidic Shakti is Ishtha Devata. This name became blended in India to create Ishvari, the "Queen of All," whose name then spread to Mesopotamia where She was worshipped as Ishtar, Astarte, and Ashtoreth, and despised in the Old Testament of the Bible as Asteroth. Shiva is also called Ishana ("Sovereign") in India, which may well have been taken as His female aspect in the Near East as Inanna; and He is called Hara, which may have been the derivation for the Goddess Ishara. As "The Lord" united with the Goddess, Shiva is Isha to Shakti's Uma in modern Tantric expressions of Shivaism, so the God's name enters into both feminine and masculine forms. This confusing of male Shiva as female is understandable when one remembers that He is also the Divine Androgyne. Western historians had a problem deciding whether to call Shiva male or female until further study of Hinduism brought them to realize that Shakti was Shiva's other half. Older writings sometimes display this misunderstanding by referring to Shiva in the feminine gender.

The name Shiva is preserved in the Judaic tradition as the word for the Talmudic school for training the rabbi, "Yeshiva" ("a sitting"). This is Dravidic Shiva as Teacher, Shiva Yogi. Shiva can also be found in the name of a Judaic calendar month, and the term for mourning. Ishtar has been renovated as Esther and made into a proper Jewish maiden, while the mourning term for Shiva was possibly derived from the earlier Aryan myth that placed Him as one who haunts the burning places of cremations.

The Trinity of the Godhead encompassed by the Great Goddess.

The Vedic Aryans had attempted to end worship of Dravidic Shiva by associating Him with their own deity, Rudra, the "Howler," a God of aversion to be feared and placated rather than adored. The rivalry between Shiva and the Fire Gods of the Vedic Aryans was clearly present, and continued until Shiva finally became accepted as the third part of a new Hindu Trinity, displacing Indus and lessening the power of the God of Fire, Agni. O'Flaherty's study of the series of myths dealing with Shiva and Agni show that even the Fire God could not stand against the "fire" of procreation. When sent by Brahma to spy upon Shiva and Parvati making love, he was spotted, and Shiva had Agni consume His semen. The result was that Agni, the revered Fire God who symbolized the power of the Vedic Aryans, could not contain the Fire of Life and spat it into the Ganges. The river could not contain it either, and tossed it into the reeds, and from there came Shiva's son Skanda, the God of War. There are a number of tender Hindu myths and depictions of Shiva as a gentle father to Skanda, so that Shiva's fierce Vedic aspect in Hinduism was always mitigated by His Dravidic loving aspect. The Dravidic power of love was stronger than the Aryan power of fire.

Shiva, being a deity who is very approachable by men and women alike on a personal basis, without the need of an intervening priesthood, was not acceptable to the Aryans who created the Judaic system. The whole purpose of the Bible, then, is to support the need for a clergy who have personal contact with God and can perform feats of magic to prove that connection; yet if those same deeds are performed by other people, the magic is labeled as evil. If one looks dispassionately at the battle between the Jewish Moses and the magicians of the Pharaoh, as an example, the real lesson is not that the Jewish God was more powerful, but that these "miracles" were commonplace magic techniques worthy of any modern magician, from the Great Kreskin to David Copperfield.

The Christianization of the Judaic religious tradition resulted in a new reblending of the two versions of religion: natural and political. The European Pagan Mother Goddess is revealed as Mary, the Mother of God, and the titles and adulations that once adorned the Goddess now belong to the Virgin Mary. As Queen of the Universe, She liberates Her devotees from fear, suffering, and evil. Catholic faith states that if one prays to Her with the Rosary (prayer beads being an ancient form of Shiva worship), She will be with Her devotee at death to ease the departed into the next life. This is literally true in Pagan theology, for Mary is both Shakti and Kali. The ancient European Pagan processions and feasts dedicated to the Goddess have become those of Mary, and like the Goddess, She is associated with the elements of Water and Earth. The Vedic Hindu tradition grants that Shakti incarnates in different ages, and so it would not be difficult to consider Mary as an example of this mythological motif being redirected in early Christian times.

The influence of Sind is barely recognized in the Westernized Aryan faith that has come down to modern times. Shiva's dance is the visualization of an ancient concept only recently understood by science—that of the periodic dissolution and recreation of all life. This ceases to be disturbing when one realizes that one is fully and completely part of the process, naturally, and that neither fear nor salvation is necessary because of Grace and Power. It is the Indian idea of Oneness with God that is aspired to by Western religions, but hindered by a preoccupation with segregating Christian believers into groups of "saved and unsaved"; "them and us." Not only have rivalries between groups of Christians been a continuous problem, but the rejection of non-Christian beliefs has resulted in an intolerance that fuels greater segregation and hostility, so that the Christian faith itself is both at war with its external competition and its internal components. This has allowed the faith to become fragmented by the ideas of various leaders and religious thinkers attempting to impose their own interpretations of beliefs on others. Fears over who would survive the dissolution of the Universe have led to unnecessary hatreds, resentments, and war—unnecessary because science has already proved that everyone ultimately survives since energy cannot be destroyed, but simply continues to exist—*it is,* just as Shiva *is.*

The Christian religion echoes the Judaic tradition with its insistence that people have an inborn guilt, but carries this further with the threat of a final judgment and eternal punishment. This atmosphere of terror is spurred, not by murders or rapes or slaughters of war, which have been commanded, sometimes in sickening detail, by the Aryan God numerous times in the Bible, but by natural human sexuality. God, then, is not offended by bloodshed and the degradation of people, but by the penis and the vagina, yet He is supposed to have created humanity and chosen its forms.

The Aryan disapproval of the phallic elements of the Old Religion did not prevent these from being incorporated into the newer versions, however. In Egypt, the severed sexual organs of Osiris were honored in special rites involving wooden replicas, and Danielou states that in Italy the "holy foreskin" of Christ is still venerated. The word linga means "distinctive sign," and thus even formless objects in which the presence of the Divine is felt can be called by this word. Danielou sees this association in the many localized traditions of pillars and rough stones, tree stumps and megaliths, and in the Black Stone of Islamic veneration at Mecca.

The element of deity castration, either actual as by removal of the sexual organs entirely, or symbolic as by circumcision, is an Aryan characteristic that does not apply to Dravidic Shiva, whose emblem is the erect phallus. Shiva is unashamedly sexual and generative—He is both uninhibited Pleasure and Life. Shivan mythology makes it clear that the only men who fight against natural sexuality do so because of their feelings of inadequacy before the source of the Universe. The need for Aryan-based religions to emasculate the phallic aspect of the Divine stems from the subordination of the earliest religious form inherent in Aryan beliefs (covered in more detail later). In order to establish the impotent political deities, the sexual deities of nature had to be castrated— Jesus could be seen as the most successful outgrowth of this practice, since He represents the normally ithyphallic Shiva as a nonsexual being in Christianity. The Son of God personally has no sexual practices, no sexual associations, no sexual references, and no sexual desires—not because of His divinity, but because His divine father is the Aryan Lawgiver rather than the Dravidic Creator of Heaven and Earth.

It becomes apparent as one studies the Bible that there are two different kinds of God in this literature. One deity, as Danielou and Toynbee view the matter, is a creative First Cause, but the other, more prevalent one, appears based on a typical local village deity who worries over such mundane things as whether or not the civil and dietary laws are observed, and whether or not people are holding to the rules of the Sabbath. Again, this shows the difference between the original God of Sind, Shiva as the creator and author of life through the Goddess, and the overlapping of the much later Aryan invention of a political God of the Law and Wrath.

In the Dravidic tradition, devotion is a personal matter and an individual responsibility (which is actually the case whether one is a member of a religious organization or not), for beliefs are internal. The very understanding of orthodox theology is unique to each individual, no matter how similar the rituals enacted while functioning within a group. It was not until the rise of rulers and their warriors that the Godhead was changed, and a religious orthodoxy and hierarchy were created to theologically support the new secular reality of a class structure. This privileged status of clerical representatives before God is an Aryan innovation whose original purpose has long been outlived. The world order is moving toward more elected representation in governments, and this may well fuel a religious reconstruction that will reflect the more recent secular reality.

The problem with social change is that it causes upheaval and unrest. People become alarmed and then scapegoats are found to alleviate the difficulty of this new passage. It was social change that instigated the Salem Witch hunts, brought into action the Ku Klux Klan, made the Red Scare (the Cold War, beginning early in the 1950s) a factor in American life, allowed Senator Joseph McCarthy and McCarthyism to thrive, drew people into cults like that of Jim Jones in the 1960s and 1970s and more recently the Branch Davidian followers of David Koresh, and has spawned the current rash of Fundamentalism throughout the world. The "Doomsday Churches" of Korea got their power over thousands of people because of the social changes affecting South Korea and the possibility of unification with North Korea. When the end of the world fails to appear for such churches, be it the Korean ones or the Jehovah's Witnesses or others in America (who have had several "end dates" pass), the explanation is always the same—someone misunderstood what God said, but never mind, the Second Coming and the end of the world are really just around the corner. And so they have been since Christianity first started, with hysteria rising at every crisis and every millennium. How much more of this nonsensical and self-destructive behavior people will accept before dealing with changes in a rational manner is unpredictable, but the grip of the clergy on the minds of the populace must be shown for the power play that it is.

Once people understand the source of religion, the terror it holds will dissipate. The result may be a genuinely new form of Paganism, one in which individuals take back responsibility for their actions, decide whether or not they will hold religious observances, and determine their own rites based on need and appropriateness under societal laws which they themselves create through representative government. One must come to terms with reality. The time for a purely upper-level Aryan religion has passed, just as has the time of a pure Dravidic religion. The social structure that Aryan religion supported is no longer there in many nations, and so the power structure of the religion remains as a skeletal brace standing on its own without true purpose, except to perpetuate its mythology for self-preservation. Neo-Paganism is at its best when taking the wheat of the past and discarding the chaff.

The power shift will likely be fought by organized clergies of the world, and already, emotional and militant terrorism are the weapons of choice, for in matters of faith there seldom have been any other weapons. Reason, knowledge, and accessibility of information are the enemies of an orthodox priesthood, and with the age of instant communication already begun, the first goal must be the alienation and isolation of the believers. This is evident in Iran and it is accomplished through various church-run schools in Europe and America, wherein children are educated from the nursery level through college in a distorted environment of religious fervor and social separation. The media itself becomes the target, accused of being a carrier of heresy and a purveyor of evil. Censorship is one method of controlling what goes through the media; another method is to deprive the source of its funding, hence the recent attempts by Fundamentalist groups in America to have the funding of Public Television eliminated because it presents unorthodox programming that dares to contradict religious teachings.

Once a unity of purpose exists between nations, based on an understanding of each other's needs for security, the fomenters of religious terrorism will be brought to bay. The world is currently experiencing the travails of a progress in which religion is in competition with numerous sciences, while simultaneously being exposed as mythology by archaeologists. There have been a number of well-produced educational programs on television, usually limited to the cable channels, concerning the new discoveries in archaeology. Even when a pseudo-scientific program is patently trying to establish that "Eve" was a reality and that genetic studies and theories "prove" that all life came from the Near East or Africa, the truth cannot remain hidden. Two weeks after just such a Fall 1992 program on Neanderthal and Cro-Magnon man in Judea, new anthropological evidence was discovered in Europe that completely negated the conclusions of the show about the truth of the Bible story. The continuing improvements in scientific research and archaeological techniques are opening up new vistas in the understanding of human history as a functioning part of the Earth's dynamics. Yet creationism and evolution are still being debated for inclusion in some public school curriculums.

Changes in perceptions about the Earth, the Universe, and life itself are being felt in most societies, and any power structure based on ignorance and dogmatic interpretation will naturally suffer. It is only a matter of time before the strangulation grip of organized religions is removed from the throat of human societies. Then perhaps people will be free to care for one another in a mutually beneficial and nonjudgmental manner.

Of Wicca and Fairies

Klostermaier and Durant, along with a host of other historians, agree that the Aryan invaders arrived in waves beginning around 2150 B.C.E. This would then result in the Dravidians fleeing from the conquerors as they swept in from the northwest and west, slowly pushing their way eastward across the valley toward the great cities near the Indus River. The refugees of the western and northern regions migrated in various directions, one of which was into Southern India. By 1600 B.C.E., the cities of Sind were feeling the pressure of Aryan encroachment, entering into a period of decline which culminated with the fall of the cities in 1200 B.C.E. During this time, the Great Goddess of the Dravidians was known by the name Danu. She would give birth to Her Son, whom She wed upon maturation; He impregnated Her with Himself, died, and was reborn at Winter Solstice. This is the typical religious mystery of agricultural society. Snakes and cows were associated with Danu and Her Son, Vritra, as they had/have been with their antecedents and successors, Shakti and Shiva.

Stone relates the Hindu myth of the murder of Danu and Vritra by Indra (to gain supremacy, which lasted until Indra was deposed by Shiva) with the Mesopotamian myth of Anu, the Indo-European sky god. This myth dates to circa 1600–1400 B.C.E. and tells of the unsuccessful attempt to kill the Great Goddess and Her

Son. When one recalls how Hindu mythology tends to be restated with different endings, one can see a merging of Danu and Anu with respect to the Sind deities. Danielou relates the God Anu to Shiva, and by examining the routes laid out by Klostermaier for Dravidic dispersion, reaching into Sri Lanka and Indonesia, and remembering that the Dravidians were noted sailors, one can be led to associate these worshippers of Danu/Anu with the aborigines of Japan, the so-called "Hairy Ainu." The Ainu were later displaced by the people now called the Japanese, who arrived from Manchuria.

One can also see the possibility of Dravidians sailing across the Pacific Ocean to settle on Easter Island when one realizes, as Basham points out, that the picto-writing of the people of Easter Island, who were dubbed the Long-Ears, matches that of Mohenjo-daro. Shiva is usually depicted with long ears, and although His ears sometimes have rings or holes for earplugs, there are usually no ornaments present, or else flowers are indicated. The Dravidians may have progressed as far as Peru, based upon the connection made by Norwegian archaeologist Thor Heyerdahl between the Long-Ears and Peruvians, although he was initially working from the other direction. At that time, he did not know of the matching picto-writing.

The masterful irrigation systems of Peru predate the Incas, and this is a technique first seen in the Indus Valley, thus lending yet another connection between these people. The facility of the mysterious Anasazi of Mesa Verde in North America with irrigation techniques and their apparent differences from Native North American tribes, who refer to these people as "Ancient Ones" rather than as ancestors, could indicate a link with the Dravidians. The name itself is reminiscent of the people of Sind identified by Danielou as "adivasi" ("first inhabitants") and who S. S. Sarkar, in *Aboriginal Races of India*, identified as the most ancient surviving race of humankind, pre-dating the Negroid, and as having Neanderthal connections. Again, irrigation is a feature of these unknown people, and when they disappeared so did the technique in North America. The development of Native American tales about a "fairie people" could relate then to similar tales which appeared in Europe. When the Fairie Folk are discussed later on, one might want to consider whether or not there might be a link. If the Anasazi were indeed related to the people of the Indus, then they were colonists who eventually met with ill luck. The Long-Ears were killed and eaten by the Short-Ears, who were the local inhabitants of Easter Island before the arrival of the Long-Ears. The Peruvians Heyerdahl associates with the Long-Ears were driven out of Peru. And the Anasazi prospered for a time and then simply vanished in a manner evocative of the Irish Fairie folk.

The Dravidians had another route they could take, however, and that was westward, across Anatolia (Turkey), into Eastern Europe, across the Mediterranean, and into Western Europe and the British Isles. As Hawkes relates, one of their primary exports was their religion, and so wherever they traveled, they took their religious customs with them. Just as the Aryans invaded in waves, so the Dravidians migrated in a series of waves, starting in 2100 B.C.E. and persisting until after 1250 B.C.E., while the Aryan invaders were moving across Sind in stages over the centuries. Charles Picard, in his work, *The Pre-Hellenic Religions* (as quoted in Danielou), indicates that there was a substratum of foreign words in the Greek language whose origins relate to those of Dravidic Sind, and that the people of Minos, the center of the first Greek civilization, said of themselves that they were not Greek.

Later-arriving Dravidians brought with them some of the Aryan Hindu mythology that had been incorporated into the myths of those Dravidians who dwelled in the perimeter areas controlled by the Aryans, and so it was that the myth of Daksha can be found in both Europe and India. This myth concerned the Aryan primal Father God whose daughter, Sati, wed Shiva against Her father's permission. He gave a sacrifice for all the Gods of Hinduism, but excluded Shiva. Sati threw Herself into the fire to be Her husband's offering so He would not be dishonored, and Shiva, naturally enraged, took the entire sacrifice and beheaded Daksha. Klostermaier, in his work, "The Original Daksha Saga," published in the

Journal of South Asian Literature, (Vol. 20, No. 1 of 1985, p. 93–107) believes that this myth relates to an actual battle wherein the people of Sind defeated the Aryans and retook territory. The myth, however, does not end there. Shiva relented and restored Daksha to life, who then became a devotee of Shiva, and He gave Daksha the head of a goat to replace the one cut off.

While this myth may relate to a small reconquest by the Dravidians and the eventual blending of the two peoples and their faiths, it also shows that the Dravidians were made to set aside the worship of their Great Goddess, Shakti, in order to retain the veneration of their God, Shiva. Shakti is depicted as willingly stepping aside for the sake of Her Consort and Her followers, for to worship Shiva is to worship Shakti—They are One. The Aryan deity, Daksha, is frequently portrayed with a goat's head, and it is from this image that Baphomet, the enthroned goat-headed god of the Knights Templar, was derived. This was an attempt by these knights, who lived in the Near East and absorbed some knowledge of the past, to restore Aryanism during the Middle Ages. Baphomet was their image of the Aryan "God the Father." This would not be the first nor the last effort to purify Aryanism in Europe. The figure of Baphomet/ Daksha has since become the image of Satan, which is ironic, since this is the same Aryan deity who would become the Creator in the Old Testament of the Bible, and God the Father in the New Testament. The cosmological injunction that the devil is God reversed continues to be a theological problem in developing a purely upper level Aryanism. It is interesting that the Council of Toledo in 447 C.E. delineated the appearance of the devil that merged the typical pre-Christian Horned God image with that of Daksha.

Historians have noted that a Scandinavian rock carving of a figure with a horned head and two hammers has been dated to the Bronze Age, but that this divinity predates belief in Thor. The wearing of a horned helmet may have developed from an earlier custom of wearing the skin of an animal with the horns still attached as a means of gaining that animal's perceived power. Horns have also been transferred in art and religion to non-horned creatures like

Baphomet
(This image of Baphomet was created by Eliphas Levi, circa 1856.)

snakes in places as far apart as Greece, China, and Mexico, which could be an indication of contact between these people. The Horned God of Sind is the oldest known example of such a deity and has been for 30,000 years the god of a historically ancient manufacturing and merchant people who had extensive trade routes by sea.

In Judaic tradition, Moses is described as being horned after receiving the Ten Commandments, although modern translators of the Bible found this disturbing and changed the meaning to having light coming from his head. The early Christian paintings and sculpture (including the famous stone portrait created by Michelangelo), working from the original version of the orthodox Christian Scriptures, portray Moses with horns. The dispute between Aaron and Moses is believed by some historians to represent a feud between two groups of bull and snake worshippers. Moses himself is supposed to have set up a bronze snake on a pole for the Hebrews to worship, and it is described as having remained in the temple for many generations. But again, one must keep track of the differences between history and mythology. Horns and snakes are emblems of Shiva, not Aryans. Durant, while using the Bible as a historical tool in discussing Judea, admitted that he did so only because there was no other evidence to work with at that time. He also concedes that the Bible stories of Moses were not written until after the preachings of Amos and Isaiah, who do not even mention Moses, and in this way he betrays his own source as suspect. The only value of mentioning the Bible stories of Moses here is to show the Horned God attributes of Moses and to note that these were eliminated by modern Christian interpreters of the Bible in art and in the teachings of the Fundamentalists.

It is a mistake to think that ancient people did not know about each other, for the evidence indicates just the opposite. The Japanese and Chinese, for example, not only knew about the Pacific Northwest Native Americans, they either conducted trade with them or were washed ashore by storms as long ago as 10,000 B.C.E., according to recent archaeological discoveries at a 12,000-year-old Indian site in the state of Washington. Since Shiva was being depicted by 28,000

B.C.E. with the horns of a bull, and the bull was sacred to Him, it could be that the symbolism spread to Europe during trade exchanges, for the merchants of Sind traveled throughout the Near East and the Mediterranean regions. Indeed, the fearsome minotaur can be seen in India as late as the tenth century C.E. in temple carvings at Khjuraho, expressing part of the living tradition of Dravidic Shiva. The cave paintings of the Indus Valley are 10,000 years older than those of Europe, and the receding ice of the last Ice Age may have encouraged people from the Indus to migrate toward what is now Europe, or at least to begin contacting whatever indigenous European tribes existed there.

It is possible, too, that the Green Wicca of Northern European peoples actually got its start from early contacts with the Indus people. The matter remains one of speculation until archaeology makes further discoveries, but as the Indus area was producing signs of civilization 10,000 years before Europe, and Europe developed the same sort of early correlations in regard to deities and horned animals as in the Indus, one could assume that either this is a normal evolution of human beliefs, or there was contact between these two regions. The divergence in customs only comes with the development of a ruling and warrior class system a little over 4,000 years ago, leading to layering in Europe and merging in the Indus. The real change in Western religion did not occur until the collapse of the Roman political structure and its replacement by the Catholic religious one, and after that it still took several centuries to eliminate the pre-Christian religion as a viable rival.

The Dravidians, migrating away from Sind with the early Aryan invasions, have been identified by some historians, such as Danielou and Ross, as either related to or at least influential on the Bronze Age Etruscans. Herodotus ascribes to the Etruscans an origin in Lydia (in Anatolia), arriving in Italy by the sea, and Massa, in *The World of the Etruscans*, uses mythic comparisons that agree and suggest that there were waves of these migrations. The Etruscans established a confederation of twelve cities, and survived for some seven centuries after appearing around 1200 B.C.E.—the same time as the Aryan push through Asia Minor and into the Near East. They were eventually diminished until falling under Roman domination in the third century B.C.E. Massa believes that the Eastern influence evident in Etruria was eventually superceded by the Greeks. The decorative motifs were Asian and included Indian lotuses and tigers, while the style of dress was also typical of Asia.

The Etruscans loved to dance and enjoyed life. Music was very important to them, and they led their hunts with flute-players. The contemporary writer, Elienus, said that the sounds of the flutes broke into the silence over the hills and in the woods, mesmerizing the animals, who then left their lairs. Much of what has been written about the Etruscans is reminiscent of traditional fairie legends. The women were equals with the men and participated in business and public life. Husbands and wives and their children are depicted in numerous paintings and sculpture as smiling and with arms linked or holding hands. Such displays of affection were unusual to the Greeks and Romans who were, as described by fourth century B.C.E. Greek historian, Theopompus, astonished by this and by the casual attitude of the Etruscans toward nudity and sexuality, with public sexual unions

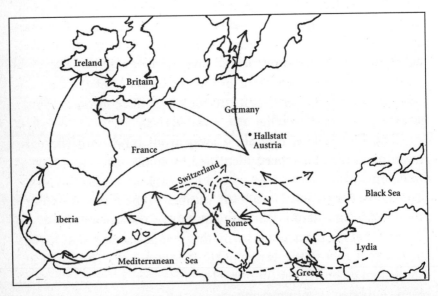

Etruscan and Celtic Migrations

not unusual. He wrote that the women paid great attention to their grooming, engaged in gymnastics with men while skimpily dressed, enjoyed parties and drinking with anyone, and did not know or care who fathered their children. He claimed that male and female prostitutes were readily available (although Massa believes this more of a misinterpretation—the word prostitute connoting something different from the reality—much as Stone has suggested that the so-called harlots of the Bible were performing religious duties), and that the couples made love watching one another after banquets. Plautus, Horace, and Aristotle accepted such stories as the truth, and while there may have been some exaggeration, the wall paintings of the Etruscans show a definite love of life and living well.

Like the Dravidians, these people honored the Horned God, depicted and interpreted now as Pan with his pipes, and had images of the phallus everywhere. The Etruscans, as Massa points out, were builders of fortified cities with sewer networks, drainage channels, and a system of irrigation in the Chiana valley. It was the Etruscans who built the great sewer of Rome. Again, this is characteristic of the Sind civilization. They were skilled with arches and bridges, and they usually decorated their archways with what has variously been called a human face, a Gorgon mask, or a foliate face. With the Roman conquest of the Etruscans, some survivors were assimilated into Roman society, but others fled into the mountains and beyond.

The Romans destroyed most of the Etruscan culture, but took many symbols and ideas from them (they left no writings themselves), and some of these appear similar to what was in Sind. The face commonly used by the Etruscans became typical in Roman art and was known as the Face of Truth. It is an image that is usually seen on wall or fountain plaques throughout Italy even today, and is a fearsome visage with a gaping mouth, surrounded by wavy hair and beard so as to look rather like a lion or a sunburst. The face does not actually relate to classical mythology, and Durant merely remarks that its origin has been lost in the mists of time. Its origin is, however, not lost when one realizes that it is surprisingly accurate in relation to a myth about Shiva.

In the Shiva myth, a demon had created an army and attacked the Vedic Gods. When Brahma and Vishnu realized they were about to be overwhelmed, they pleaded with Shiva to help them. The demon mounted his attack against Shiva, but the God simply opened His third eye and created a fiery creature who devoured the entire army. The demon leader saw this and begged Shiva for mercy. The God never turns away a petitioner, and so He spared the demon leader, who then became a devotee of Shiva. But the monster also prayed to Shiva, saying that as He had created it hungry, He must give it something more to eat. Shiva told the creature to eat itself, and it faithfully complied, devouring itself from the feet up until all that remained was the maned face with its open mouth. Shiva was so pleased that He caused this image to be placed at the entry to all His temples, for the Hungry Face is testimony to the truth that all life feeds on life, and in this sense, life feeds on death by the consumption of other life. Until one accepts this, one cannot know Shiva, and from this concept came both the Mediterranean symbol and its name, the Face of Truth, or Face of Glory.

Since the early days of Aryan expansion, the Pagan system of Europe had been undergoing a division, or layering, of belief systems. The Pagans of Europe had a multileveled system that reflected the class of the worshipper. Edred Thorsson, in his book, *Northern Magic: Mysteries of the Norse, Germans, and English,* describes the system as composed of the Chief (or King) and the Warriors placed on the pinnacle of a three-tiered triangle, with their great deities being a Father God, a Lawgiver, and a Warrior God. These deities had different names, depending on the location. The masses were left with the earliest form of European Paganism, which was called Green Wicca in the Teutonic system. This was the worship of the God and the Goddess as equals, or twins, and the practice of magic with herbs and natural substances, and shamanic union with the Universal Energy to effect magic and gain wisdom. When Dravidian refugees from Sind began to arrive in Europe, their practices and beliefs found them a place in the base-level of the Teutonic pyramid of deities and their respective realms. Shiva and Shakti were easily equated with Frey and Freya (which simply mean "Lord and Lady"), and the assimilation of the religion of Sind into that of the European lower classes resulted in an evolving of the Green level into what is today called Wicca ("The Wise"), or Witchcraft ("Craft of the Wise").

Freya (as depicted on a Tarot card)

The people of Sind combined with the Europeans, forming the modern anthropological type that is commonly called Indo-European, and their religious practices blended together nearly 3,000 years ago to form a revitalized Wiccan tradition. It is not difficult to trace many Wiccan practices back to their origins in the religion of Shiva and Shakti. The idea of being "sky-clad" (naked) in ritual gatherings comes from the worship of Shiva as Digambara ("Sky-Clad," or "Clothed in Space"). The cards and suits of the Tarot (and suits of modern playing cards) come from the accouterments of Shakti as Durga—trident (rods, wands, clubs), sword (sword, spades), drum (cup, hearts), and bowl (dish, pentacles, diamonds). The Major Arcanum of the Tarot was derived from the various aspects of Shiva and Shakti (the Fool, for example, being one of Shiva's aspects in the shamanic sense of being unperturbed when beginning the quest that is a new cycle of life). Many people believe that the Tarot is an Egyptian creation, while others feel that the cards actually came from the Gypsies, who were mistakenly labeled Egyptians. Their current name, Gypsies, is derived from Egyptian, but historians and anthropologists recognize that they were actually from India. This information can be found in any number of

A Gypsy Encampment in Syria

history texts, but is only one piece of the whole which, when placed in perspective, presents a different view of the growth of religions. The Gypsies, then, are the direct descendants of the Dravidians of the Indus, and the primary carriers of the Old Religion into Medieval Christian Europe.

The use of a Craft Name in Wicca comes from the same practice used by devotees of Shiva. This has been copied in the Roman Catholic Church with a new name being assigned to the devotee at the confirmation ceremony, thus designating this person as now capable of receiving the sacraments. For the Shivaite, Klostermaier reports, the new name is one that signifies the Supreme Deity, whereas most Catholic names of confirmands are selected from a list of saints or angels. With the solitary witch, the craft name may be of any type and is the name by which the person is known among other practitioners, and a working name is one revealed by the Deities, used in the performance of magic and kept secret. In the case of the Shivaite, the Roman Catholic, and the Wiccan, the name is stated by the leader (guru, priest, or priestess) and the initiate is welcomed into the congregation—or circle—by that name.

The Pagan concept of the cauldron of life producing the life of the Earth, referred to as the womb of the Goddess, is related to the Yoni of the Dravidic system. Like the Yoni, the energy of life is given its form through the cauldron of the Pagan deities. When one's life is over, one goes back into the cauldron to be reborn; thus there is no end to the bounty thereof. Again there is a similarity of beliefs that would allow for a merging of cultures into what would become modern Wicca. It is because of this that Wicca is likely to be much more true to the original religion of Sind than what can be distilled from modern Hinduism. The names of the deities may have been altered to reflect European culture, but the identity remains intact. The Triple Goddess is still Shakti, and the Horned God is still Shiva, who is named in India, Shiva Tryambaka ("Wed to the Triple Goddess"). A living religion changes with time and evolves with the civilization it is centered in, and so the deities of Sind have also changed. Just as the Christianity of modern America is not the

Christianity of the 4th Century C.E. Stylites (people who sat atop poles in the wilderness for many years as a testament of their faith, and who became saints—somewhat like the practicing of austerities by Hindu Yogis), the Wicca of today is not the same as that of the Middle Ages.

The characterization of Hecate and the Morrigu can be found in the Dravidian tradition to this day. Without Shiva, Shakti is presented in the aspect of Dhumavati ("The Crone"), representing the dark forces and black magic, and portrayed as a crow. From the Indus point of view, this is unenergized energy—ugly and unorganized in form. Shiva without Shakti is energy without expression, so it is only together that they function properly. They need each other for vibrant power, and this duality is implicit in Their worship. Yet as the Goddess of Power, it was Shakti that dominated the religion carried to Ireland and later merged with that of the Celts. The name, Morrigu or Morrigan, Goddess of War for the Celts, can be seen as related to Mururgan, the War God of the Tamils of India. The Tamils are an ethnic people whom Klostermaier believes to be directly descended from the Dravidians of Sind, and so their beliefs are often used as a guide for those of pre-Vedic India. Mururgan is worshiped with a frenzied dance, and His weapon is the spear.

The Dravidic Tamils also venerate a War Goddess, Korravai, whose name might have evolved, over the centuries in the British Isles, to become Cerridwen. Since the Tamils of Southern India are believed to have descended from the refugees who fled the Indus Valley during the Aryan invasions, it is possible that others took flight by ship and sailed to Ireland, becoming the Fir Bolg of legend. They were subsequently conquered by a later-arriving group of Dravidians (circa 1500 B.C.E.), the Tuatha de Danu—whose name is Sanskrit for "People of the Goddess Danu." Danu is described in Aryan texts as a Tree Goddess, and is an aspect of Devi/Shakti that was popular in Sind between 1600 B.C.E. and 1200 B.C.E., at the time of the final conquest of the region by the Aryans.

The influence of the religion of Sind upon the development of Wicca can be seen most clearly in the Celtic tradition. The Gaelic

Celts who settled in the British Isles displaced the earlier peoples, but were most likely related to them. Some of the early legends of Pagan Ireland can be traced to Shiva. The tale of Cuchulainn and the killing of his son by the Gae Bolg repeats the legend of the death of Andhaka (who was created when a drop of Parvati's sweat fell into Shiva's third eye). Andhaka fell in love with his mother, and Shiva impaled His son on His trident—just as Cuchulainn impaled his son on the trident his fairie father had given him (the emblem of the god of a Dravidian father made as a gift to his Celtic son). Shiva, however, then burned His son to ash with His third eye, in order to restore him as purified. Today, the scattered myths of Shiva retained

The Green Man, also known as the Horned God

in the Hindu religion refer to one another, so most historians believe that at one time there was a single connected mythology which was subsequently subdivided and repeatedly revised by the Aryans. The blending that occurred in Europe may actually provide a clearer view of the original religion of Sind than the contradictory progression of myths in Hinduism.

The veneration of the Sun and Moon, trees, animals, and snakes is characteristic of the Tamils and the Tuatha de Danu who defeated the Fir Bolg, and these elements are also part of the Celtic religion. All these peoples were quite possibly related to the Dravidians of Sind, who migrated in waves toward Europe over a period of nearly 2,000 years. The color of mourning for Shivaites and Celts alike is saffron yellow, and the burial techniques are the same. Red ochre, too, is a color signifying the rebirth of life, and is used to cover the bodies of the dead.

What can be determined from the evidence is that Wicca in Europe developed from the merging of the Green Wiccan Paganism (worshipping the Lord and Lady; God and Goddess) with the religion of Sind. The Triple Goddess motif and the symbolism of the Maiden, Mother, and Crone aspects of the Goddess; the Horned God; the Lord and Lady of the Greenwood; and the God and Goddess of Sun and Moon are all found in the worship of Shiva and Shakti. The difference between Wicca and Hinduism is that the Aryan influence, which led to the worship of Shiva and Shakti in Hinduism being one of contradictions and confused symbology, is absent in Wicca. The modern Wiccan is practicing the worship of Shiva and Shakti merged with that of the Lord and the Lady of European Paganism, in a way that is indicative of how the religion of Sind might well have evolved if not disrupted by Aryan invasions and the subsequent imposition of Vedic orthodoxy and caste.

The European tradition of Green Wicca continued to grow and evolve according to its surrounding influences. Despite the upper levels of the Aryan system, the Sind tradition continued to coexist. From Jutland of the first century B.C.E. comes the Gunderstrup Cauldron with its depiction of Cernnunos ("The Horned One"), Lord of

Celtic Cernnunos (above) **and
Indus Shiva (Mohenjo-Daro Seal)**

the Animals, that is nearly a
replica of the Dravidic seal of
Shiva, Lord of the Beasts.
Even the arrival of the new
Christian religion did not
completely wipe it out, although people are still reluc-
tant to recognize the primacy
of the religion of Shiva and
acknowledge that the rites and myths of modern religions have their
basis in Shiva, complete with the association through Dionysus of
the God born in a cave, with the sacred bull or ox nearby, His riding
upon an ass for festivals, His death, and His resurrection. The
themes were all laid out in the seasons in Sind, brought to Europe,
renewed with subsequent immigration, and adopted as a literal
truth in a religion that proceeded to stifle the message of renewed
life under the weight of dogma.

The Aryan religion of India substantially altered the religion
of Sind, and the Aryan-influenced religion of Judaism worked to
further eliminate remaining traces of the older religion; but the

Aryanism of Europe actually prepared the people to accept (at least initially) a dual practice of Christianity and Paganism. Since the religion of Odin and Thor traditionally belonged to the nobility and chiefs, the religion of the people was retained, and even infused into the new system. Thus the Wiccan festival, Ostara, honoring the Goddess Oestre, became the Christian Easter, just as with earlier Judaism, Purim had been the celebration of Esther, who was actually the same as the Wiccan, non-Aryan goddess, Oestre— Astarte, Ishtar, Ishtari Devi, Shakti. Basham sees a relation between the story of Esther as the Jewish maiden who puts aside fancy clothes to win the love of a Persian king with the purpose of saving her people, and the story of Parvati winning Shiva's love by putting aside her finery and living as an ascetic, her purpose being to save the gods from destruction by a demon by winning Shiva and having his son.

The Pagan holidays that were incorporated into the Christian religion include Easter (which is the Spring Equinox) and Christmas (which is Yule—the Winter Solstice); the two main Christian holidays therefore have nothing to do with that religion and certainly do not reflect any "new" beliefs. At the same time, the Pagan customs and practices of the country folk continued to exist, unimpeded, and at times even encouraged, by the Church. The Paganism of the European common folk was tolerated until the Church had gained sufficient power to wage successful political wars.

The apparent cynicism of those in positions of power cannot be dismissed as the interpretation of hostile outsiders, for the Church records themselves give evidence to the intrigues, poisonings, murders, and manipulations that occurred in every strata of the religious hierarchy from monks to inquisitors to bishops to cardinals to popes. Anyone who reads these documents cannot fail to wonder that *any* credibility remains for Church leaders. Yet today, too, as one scandal after another rocks the popular evangelical scene in America, Fundamentalism still garners numerous followers. Historians like Gibbon, Durant, and Romer have recognized that the entire Church structure, from the pomp and ceremony surrounding the Pope, to the names of the priestly hierarchy and divisions of Church districts, comes from the Roman Emperor before Constantine, Diocletian. It was this emperor who created unity in the already fragmenting Roman Empire through the force of his personality and his reorganization of the empire into districts, called diocese, under governing bodies of ministers—a title that remains in use today in European nations for people in important positions in civil administration.

After Diocletian retired (in Yugoslavia, for he was Slavic) and lost interest in the Empire (he lived in splendor and raised cabbages), Constantine arrived on a chaotic scene. He took the structure created by Diocletian and filled the positions with his supporters—culled from the Christian populace. He could be certain of their allegiance because their survival depended on his staying in power, but he could not depend on his potential rivals in the Pagan community. Constantine could only save the empire for the duration of his life, however. When the Roman Empire finally collapsed a century later, after a series of invasions and sackings of Rome, the Christian bureaucracy was already in position to take over the governance and administration of the lands through its clergy, and the power of the Roman Catholic Church was born. Some historians have long felt that the rules of the Church do not reflect the teachings of Jesus, but of Paul, the Jewish petty bureaucrat in a despised and deadend profession who took control of the emerging religion and imposed his own interpretations. Early on the faith ceased to be derived from what was taught by Jesus, but drew its form from what was "dreamed" by Paul.

The persecutions of Witches and Pagan priests and priestesses came about only when the Church was able to recognize *de facto* control of territory through a monarch system subservient to the Pope in theological matters (by threat of excommunication—which would result in the loss of the allegiance of the ruled subjects and lead to insurrection, and the belief in the certain damnation of the immortal soul). Then it became necessary to wage war against non-Christians so that no opportunity would occur for a Pagan ruler to come into power and negate the control of the Church. Until the time of England's King Henry VIII, the Church owned vast tracts of land, held serfs, owned manors, collected taxes, and governed land within the realms of its subservient monarchs. The countryside Pagans and their practices were tolerated in many locales until the 17th Century C.E., and then continued to exist under cover of dark and in secrecy up to modern times. Although there has been much written about the nature of the Witch trials and subsequent massacres, that discussion does not actually lie within the purview of this study. However, *The Burning Times*, a well-made video shown on cable television (it has been repeated on The Learning Channel and shown on The Discovery Channel at least once) gives a good synopsis of theories for the persecutions relating to the status of women; independent women, and women practicing medicine through herbal knowledge, being eliminated so that their subjugation by men would reflect the writings of Paul and the traditions of the Old Testament.

The difficulty in destroying the Wiccan tradition in Europe and in the New World (for these customs traveled with the settlers to North and South America) stems from the very nature of the Old Religion as contrasted with the New. There has always been some allure in being part of the Earth and the Universe, rather than a species set upon the Earth to use it and discard it in hope of a better afterlife. When one lives this life and is in balance with nature, one is connected to the whole of the life energy. The self-denying and self-despising rituals of the mainstream religions of today can only be accepted as a matter of faith—even when that faith is the unreasonable acceptance of what knowledge recognizes as false. One can only deny the beauty of life in favor of an austere lifestyle meant to influence a savior who did not exist if one is kept from the knowledge of where the concepts came from and what their purposes were. Faith, then, becomes synonymous with ignorance, and wisdom becomes Witchcraft. It is for this reason that mainstream religions frequently praise faith over knowledge and consider knowledge a "forbidden fruit" that is evil.

By the time the last refugees of Sind were arriving in Europe, their predecessors were already well assimilated into the Indo-European society, so that the newcomers were the outsiders—the Gypsies. Many of their religious practices—even when mingled with Christianity—relate to those of India. From the legends of the Sibyls—the Prophetesses of Greek tradition—comes the picture of women who were wanderers, compelled by the Sun God to speak whether they wanted to or not. These may have been the early forerunners of the Gypsy fortunetellers. The Sibyls were considered uncouth, unkempt vagabonds by Roman and Christian standards, and this is the same prejudice that remains against Gypsies in many parts of the world today. Like the Dravidians and the Hindus, the Gypsies also have a tradition of river bathing and river veneration.

While modern Wicca evolved from the merging of the Dravidic religion of Sind and the Green Wicca of the Aryans, there is one more factor to add to Wicca, and that is the element of negative reactions to Christian intolerance. From this comes the popular misconception of all Witches celebrating a Black Mass and performing degrading acts with sacred objects like the consecrated host (stolen from a Catholic mass) and the crucifix (hung upside down). This is not Witchcraft, but an anti-Christian sentiment expressed by people deliberately displaying their contempt for the stifling religion they may have been forced to publicly accept. The Black Mass and the Witch's Sabbat are *not* the same thing, although it has been convenient for mainstream religionists to treat them as though they were. The Sabbat of Witchcraft does not involve denouncing another religion, but is a celebration of human connection with the powers of the Earth and the Universe. Spellwork is not even involved at a Sabbat. Nevertheless, Christians generally will link "Satanists" with Witches as a scare tactic to prevent anyone recognizing that there is an older alternative to their religion—one that has no relation to their imagined god of evil. The Horned God is not the Evil One of Christianity—Wicca does not have an evil god. The Hell ruled by the Christian counterpart of their own God does not exist in the Wiccan tradition. The Horned God was once venerated by people as a powerful and benevolent deity for humankind, but now is feared by those who refuse to recognize that their religious heritage comes from the same root.

Back when Christianity was first getting started, there were disputes over what was doctrine and what was heresy. Learned theologians and philosophers considered various points and argued in the tradition of Jewish Rabbis over the meanings of Scriptural passages, words, and even punctuations (Edward Gibbon relates in his two volume work, *The Decline and Fall of the Roman Empire*, that one religious war in North Africa resulting in the death of over 100,000 people was based on whether or not to dot an "i", since the first transcriber had neglected to do so, and an attempt to correct this mistake was seen as heresy—the non-dotted "i"s won). At the time of the Christian foundation in Rome, the highly popular religion of Cybele and Attis was celebrated with great pomp and pageantry. Attis was the beloved youth wed to the Goddess Cybele, and like the phases of the Moon, His death, three days of darkness, and resurrection was an annual event. There would be a procession through the streets of Rome, with His image transported on a platform on the shoulders of the devout. He would be hung on a tree in accordance with the mythology, buried in a tomb, and on the third day, His followers would run through the streets of Rome with lighted tapers shouting, "He is risen!" Yet this religious activity predates Jesus and Christianity, and was an ongoing faith at the time Christians were just beginning to be identified as a group in 150 C.E. It is easy to see now where the traditions of Catholic pageants, with the parading of images through the streets, have their origins.

The confusing mixture of the traditions of Krishna, the practices associated with Cybele and Attis, the Green Wicca of European Paganism, and the missionary work of Buddhists and Shivaites in Rome, make for a strange concoction called Christian tradition. Centuries later, in 1843 C.E., the Persian prophet Mirza Husayn Ali would see the connections and deify himself and his descendants for pointing it out to his disciples. He created the

Bahai faith out of Babism ("The Gate"), a pantheistic religion that relates all faiths together as one faith, and involves abstinence from alcohol, begging, slavery, and polygamy. The curious thing about the term pantheism is that Christianity deplores the notion as somehow indicative of a primitive and inferior religion, yet the Bible speaks of God as being in all things, and the Gospels state that God dwells within a person. These are the same elements of the ancient worship of Shiva and Shakti.

Throughout Christian history, there have been attempts at refining and reconstructing the basic tenets of the faith to make the religion more clearly defined. These efforts have produced wars, persecutions, and a plethora of Christian denominations, each of which believes itself to be the only "true" religion of Jesus. The small number of faithful (as suggested by the book of Revelation) destined to be saved from the last days of Armageddon provokes this kind of irrational frenzy. If people would recognize that some aspects of the Bible are political, some mythological, and some a form of arcane cosmology, there would not be such terror and fatalism in modern life.

With the practice of modern Wicca one should expect and welcome changes, otherwise Wicca and Neo-Paganism would be archaic ritual with no real value in the modern world. Sympathetic magic is not needed for fertility in the fields; blood sacrifices and ritual strangulations are today as representational as the Christian's holy eucharist with bread and wine; there are no more "wicker men" filled with living human sacrifices (although it has been argued that this image was invented to discredit the local Druids), and no more slain messengers to the gods. The flow of energy is constant throughout history, but the evocation should be naturally updated so as to not limit human growth to an anachronism.

Religion needs to be living and vital, not limited to stagnating old practices unrelated to current scientific understanding and modern social realities. It is impossible to find a purity of religious thought in European Paganism or to refer to practices of the Old Religion prior to the disruption of Christian dominance. The only choice left is to review the history, see the roots of beliefs and how they have evolved, and select what is appropriate for this age. To hold onto misogynistic or discriminatory practices is to refuse to accept the equality of all people. If one desires to live with a sense of exclusiveness and smug superiority, one should at least have the courage to do so as a conscious fact of personality and choice, not as a follower of some ideology cloaked in religious terminology. This applies to the practice of any religion—be it an Eastern faith, a Christian denomination, or a Wiccan tradition. The purpose of religion and ritual should be to hone the spiritual aspect of people; to make them aware of their surroundings and their part in nature; to help them identify their place in the flow of the cosmic and natural forces around them so they can be at peace within, and in harmony with each other and their planet.

The Fair Folk

But where do the fairies fit in? If anyone had said fairies were real in the last century, that person would have suffered the same fate as Sir Arthur Conan Doyle's father—a quick trip to the nearest insane asylum. Today there are people involved in historical research and people in the Neo-Pagan movement who seriously approach the subject of the Fair Folk and offer explanations as to why mention is made of these mysterious beings in nearly every culture in one form or another, but usually as the "Shining Ones." Are fairies a different species, living in a parallel world, connected to this world at the ley lines of magnetic pulses, and able to travel between dimensions? Are they a people so mysterious that the only description that suits them is to say that they are "Other"? Are they the elementals in a visible form? Are they the remnants of ancient tribes, like the Picts, for example? Or are they the diminished form of ancient deities? All these ideas have been discussed in varying degrees of seriousness by Neo-Pagans, theologians, archaeologists, and historians.

The fact that historical figures—like William the Conqueror— are said to have married someone of this race suggests that there is a rational explanation for at least some aspects of the Sidhe (pronounced "Shee" or "Sheathe" with the "th" very soft). Both Cottie Burland and Alain Danielou agree that the ancient people of the Indus, small and graceful, populated Europe early in the Neolithic Age, and were either eliminated or absorbed by the stronger Cro-Magnon race.

The Sidhe are the Fairie Folk of Ireland and the source of the term Banshee, the ghostly figure of a wailing woman, sometimes washing bloody linen, that foretells a death. The nobility of the Sidhe are called the Daoine Sidhe (pronounced something like "Theena Sheathe" or "Deenay Shee"), and the whole group has been linked to the Tuatha de Danu who took Ireland from the Fir Bolgs, only to lose it centuries later (about 1000 B.C.E.) to the Milesians—the Gaelic Celts. These latter victors are traditionally held to be a people who came by sea from the Near East, by way of Spain, at a time that corresponds to soon after the final Aryan push was being completed in the Indus Valley.

The artwork of the Celts and their customs show not only that there is a link between them and the Dravidians, but also between them and the Etruscans. The deities of the Celts included the Horned God and the Snake Goddess already seen in the Indus, the Near East, and the Mediterranean. Among the statues of deities shown in *The Celtic World* by Barry Cunliffe is one of a male figure seated in a Yoga position, but described as an unknown deity. While the Celts swarmed into Eastern and Western Europe from Anatolia (modern Turkey, from where the Lydians who became the Etruscans came), across Thracia and Romania (upper Greece through Constantinople-Istanbul) and through Iberia (Spain and Portugal) and Gaul (France) from 1200 to 700 B.C.E. (directly after the fall of Mohenjo-daro and the Mycenean Empire), their point of origin was beyond the Black Sea. The cult of the skull so remarkably Celtic echoes the skull traditions of Shiva as Destroyer—even to making vessels of the skulls—and may be seen as further evidence of a relationship between the Celts and the Dravidic people, whose deity by this time had been given the characteristics of the Aryan Rudra.

Then, too, the very name of the "People of Danu" is Sanskrit. Danu is the Goddess of the Fairie Folk, and is in the Dravidic tradition both a Goddess of Plenty and a devourer of humans—the Parvati and Kali aspects of Shakti. Brigit, Goddess of Knowledge, is an aspect of Danu, and is still venerated today as the Catholic Saint Brigit. In Sweden, the name of the sacred sites, *nysa,* is also the name of the Fairy Folk, the Elves or Nyssa. And Mount Nysa, of course, was where the Greek version of Shiva—Dionysus—created the festivals of the Bacchantes. The source for these names is Nisah, which means "supreme" and is an appellation of Shiva. The traditional aversion of the Fairie Folk to iron, the metal whose name may be derived from "Aryan" (Durant states that they possessed it first), would be natural for a Bronze Age people pushed from their homeland by the superior weaponry of their enemies. The magic of the Fairie Folk, the illusion sometimes called "glamour," is a characteristic found frequently in the Shiva mythology. He enjoys tricking the proud and the arrogant by appearing first as they want to see Him, only to later show them that while He is the Supreme Deity He is not lavish in dress nor opulent in taste. Only Parvati sees Him as He is when others are deluded, and only the faithful recognize that His Divinity surpasses the laws and regulations of the Vedas. Already one can see the direction this investigation is heading, and as the evidence piles up, the picture that emerges completes the circle.

The Sidhe apparently put up such a good fight that the Celts were suitably impressed and offered to give the Sidhe kings the right to live under the hills that are abundant in Ireland, although some of the Sidhe chose instead to dwell under the sea (sailed West). Today, the fairie hills are believed to have been burial mounds, but excavations are discouraged—just in case they are not. The Irish have a special feeling for the "Little People," or "Good Neighbors," and do not like anyone, especially outsiders, disturbing them. How much is mythology and how much is history? Apparently much more of the latter than most people are willing to accept.

East Gate at Sanchi
Note the spirals so often associated with Celtic artwork.

While the hovering or moving lights seen during storms or in marshy places are called fairie fire or elf light (St. Elmo's fire seen on ship's masts toward the end of electrical storms), and said to be the souls of dead warriors or children (a corpse candle), these lights are actually caused by atmospheric conditions and the ignition of gases, such as methane, emanating from decaying plant or animal matter. Yet these shining lights have been associated with the Fairies for centuries. The people of the Indus referred to the elementals as Devas—"Shining Ones"—and considered these manifestations to be neither harmful nor benevolent, but rather lesser deities or good spirits. For the Persians of 600 B.C.E., practicing the Zoroastrian religion, the Devas were demons—an example of the deities of one religion becoming the demons of another.

Historians now recognize that the people of ancient times were far more mobile than had been previously assumed. That transplanted mythologies and religious aspects of deities were widespread can be better accepted when one realizes the people sailed and traveled in caravans to the far reaches of the world. The fact that burial traditions, such as the use of red ochre to cover the deceased, are the same for Paleolithic Europeans and a people of the same time period living on the North American coast is evidence to the interaction between the two regions. The populations were not stagnant, but vibrant, engaged in trade, colonization, and exploration.

It was the Dravidian Celts, who were expert sailors, who reached Ireland by way of Spain in 1000 B.C.E., after the final stages of the Aryan invasions of the Indus Valley, displacing the Dravidian Tuatha de Danu who had come from Sind centuries before them during an earlier immigration. The very word Sidhe and the idea of such people being "of light" relates these people to Shiva. The word comes from the Sanskrit word siddha, and means "charged with energy." One becomes siddha by using words of power (mantras) of the God and the Goddess. In the case of the Tuatha de Danu, the Goddess was emphasized. These Dravidians, worshipping the aspect of Shakti as Danu, associated with trees and snakes—and becoming siddha during the recitation of mantras in religious worship—are the fairie people.

When the Celts arrived and defeated the Tuatha de Danu, they continued to hold the Tuatha in respectful deference. This was only natural since the earlier people represented a purer ethnic heritage of Sind. The worship customs of India can be found duplicated in both the Celtic religion and Celtic Fairie tradition. The offering of flowers, grain, and honey to the Goddess and the God at hilltop sanctuaries is seen in both cultures. Shiva is worshiped with gifts of milk and flowers, and this custom relates to the Celtic tradition of leaving milk for the Fairies.

The Fair Folk are also called the "Other People," and this comes from another name of Shiva. He is referred to as "Another" and "Other," and His devotees are His people—possessive, the Other's People, which in time has become the Other People. Shiva is called "Other" because He is not affected by time or eternity, nor by the creative process in which He is involved. Vedic Shiva is described as the Divine Archer, shooting His arrows indiscriminately at people, causing them to suffer death or disease, and this is the origin of the "elf shot" of the Fairie Folk. Even the name elf can be traced to

the root word "el," which Alexander Eliot, in his book, *The Universal Myths; Heroes, Gods, Tricksters and Others*, notes is the Canaanite word for "God," and which is seen in Hebrew words and landmarks such as Beth-el ("House of God"). The connection between Sind and Canaan has already been addressed, and it is possible then to link the term elf with the deities

Sacred Bull

and people of Sind. The white bull is Shiva's mount, and remained a sacred animal throughout the early civilizations of the Near East and Mediterranean, but is also retained in Celtic mythology as the form taken by two feuding deities whose heritage is Tuatha de Danu. This particular story is part of the legend of Cuchulainn and the war caused over the dun (pale) bull.

At the time of the Roman emperors there was significant commerce between India and the empire. People went to India for knowledge, and there were missionaries and emissaries from India in Rome as well as in a number of North African and Near East ern cities under the dominion of the empire. In early Christian times, the Hindus in the empire were initially scorned (Tertullian, near the end of the second century C.E., described Christians as more industrious than the Hindu people of Rome), then later they were praised (by Prosper of Aquitania several centuries later) as good examples for Christians to emulate. It is thus clear that the Hindu beliefs and deities were not unknown in the empire and were seen as an influence to be weighed when reflecting upon Christian theology. The Romans extended their empire to Britain, and Christianity obtained a foothold in the lands that were probably better associated with the religion of Sind than anywhere else in Western Europe.

When Saint Patrick went to Ireland and drove out the snakes, it was not a matter of sending reptiles slithering away from the land, but of forcing the Sidhe to leave, taking their religion of the Goddess and the God, trees and snakes, with them. The legends of early Christian Ireland make it clear that the missionaries of Christianity were greeted hospitably by the Sidhe. Charles Squire, in his book, *Celtic Myth and Legend*, shows that when the chalice of Saint Columba was repaired by the Sidhe in a gesture of friendship indicating that they would live in peaceful coexistence with the newcomer and his religion, the saint's response was one of insolence and rudeness. He cast aside the cup and stated that there could be no friendship between them unless the Sidhe converted at once, or they would suffer the consequences. The Sidhe king said that rather than do that, he would take all his people across the sea, and his curse would be upon the land he left so that it would always be a place of fighting and suffering until such time as Christian people learned courtesy toward his people. It is said that many of the Fairie Folk then sailed west, "over sea," to a new world, while others moved to Scotland and the Scottish Isles, leaving but a remnant behind.

In early Christian times the Sidhe were described as "fallen angels," too good for hell, but not good enough for heaven, because they did not choose sides in the war between God and Lucifer (the Prince of Light, from Roman times—the Morning Star; an androgyne Venus, then). The Sidhe were said to have been sent down to Earth before the creation of humans, to be the first gods of the Earth. An intriguing message is hidden in this definition (recounted by Lady Wilde in her book, *Ancient Legends of Ireland),* for it states clearly that these are *the first gods of the earth,* and that is precisely who Shiva and Shakti are. What has happened in the case of the Fair Folk is that the followers of Danu and Her Consort—the Tree Goddess and the Horned Earth God of Sind—have become identified with their deities. Today they are the beacons to the true origins of religion and may be honored for giving mute testimony through legend, myth, and history to the travels of the people of Sind in the Western world. They dwell still among us, and any who practice the Craft may claim a spiritual kindredness to them.

The religion of the Sidhe is related to the religion of the Celts and other European Pagans by virtue of having the same heritage of Sind. The Indo-Europeans are the stock of modern Western cultures, and this is because the people of the Indus traveled and took their beliefs with them. Over the millennium, the ideas of Sind were taken to the Near East and Europe, developed along similar lines in these different locations, then evolved according to the needs of the people in different regions, and came back to the source in Sind as a new form, Aryanism, only to return to the European region first as a revival of Green Wicca and then as a mixture of Aryanism and Sind in Christianity. The Horned God of the European Pagans and the modern Witch is Shiva as Lord of Beasts—the protector of the wild animals and forests. His holy places are in nature; caves, springs, mountains, and quiet, lonely places. In modern usage, He is the Lord of Shadows, the Fairie King, Oberon. As Lord of Animals, Shiva reminds people to accept their animal nature and be brethren to the creatures of the wild. In doing so, his followers become his flock, and Shiva is the Good Shepherd.

The Relationship Between
Wicca and the Teutonic System

There has sometimes been a misconception about the Northern Teutonic (Asatru) tradition, as evidenced by the description entered in Margot Adler's 1986 revision of her 1979 book, *Drawing Down the Moon*, which places it apart from other Pagan roots, such as Wicca and Druidism, and ceremonial magic. There have been charges of Nazi ties to the the Odinist version of Paganism, not all of which are unfounded, but this is addressed in the chapter about the Holocaust. Adler dwells mostly on the racial, ancestral, and conservative elements of the Teutonic religion in relation to how it functions on the level of a practiced faith. But there is a deeper level to be examined—that of the Teutonic connection with Wicca. The roots of the Teutonic are firmly entangled with those of Wicca, and the unravelling leads to a likely explanation of how that system developed. It is possible to determine where the Teutonic tradition turned from the earlier form of religious beliefs that had demonstrated either a greater equality between the sexes with a God and Goddess as Lord and Lady, or a matriarchal tendency with a Great Goddess and Her Consort. Nevertheless, in order to understand the progression from these beliefs to a dominant Father God and resulting societal class distinctions, it is necessary to consider the current format of Teutonic paganism.

The Teutonic magical system has been influential in Europe since the seventeenth century C.E., and when one looks at the Tree of Yggdrasill pattern, as depicted in Thorsson's book, the comparison to the earlier Jewish Kabbalah is readily apparent. Although there are nine rather than ten segments to the Tree, and the names vary, the one system shows the influence of the other. While Thorsson does state that Teutonic magic is not ceremonial magic (which is covered in another chapter), the timing and the historical interest in ceremonialism by German practitioners tends to blur the distinctions to some degree in modern application. During this long history of Teutonic magic, it was also involved in the Hermetic and Rosicrucian practices, but that is not the real focus of this study.

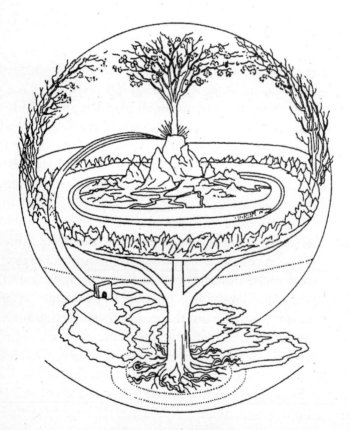

The Tree of Yggdrasill

Earlier still, Northern magic practices in general were spread throughout Western Europe by the Teutonic tribes of Vandals, Goths, Lombards, and Visigoths, so that even the Mediterranean areas of Spain, Portugal, and Italy were affected, particularly after the Roman Empire had collapsed, about 476 C.E. One must remember that the Northern tradition is itself composed of four branches—Gothic, Scandinavian, Anglo-Saxon, and German. There are various kinds of Teutonic magic and practitioners, the main two being *galster* (which is Runic) and *seidhr* (which is basically traditional Witchcraft), but both are called *vitki* ("wise one"), from which, Thorsson contends, comes the Anglo-Saxon term Wicca or Witch. The Teutons are basically Solitary Practitioners, and this in itself adds to the validity of the lone Practitioner of the craft, sometimes questioned by covens following traditions of initiations and degrees.

In Teutonic mythology, the World-Tree, called Yggdrasill, consists of nine worlds, realms, or homes, only two of which need be discussed here—those forming the two homes of the Northern deities. There is the realm called Asgard, the home of the Aesir, in particular Odin (Woden), who rules the Gods and Goddesses of all the realms, and the realm called Wane-Home, home of the Vanir, in particular Freya and Frey. In between these two structures of the deities lies the Warrior Class—under the direction of Thor, known for his hammer and called the Thunderer. The Goddess Freya and Odin may travel to each other's realms, and each is renowned for magical skill. The Aesir Gods, Odin and Tyr, represent Runic magic and law respectively, and are associated with the colors blue and white accordingly. Thor represents strength and is associated with the color red (as is Mars). Frey and Freya are twins who represent production, wealth, love, and peace, and are associated with the color green.

"Green" Wicca, then, represents the primal force of the Northern religion with its emphasis on the Lord and the Lady (Frey and Freya, literally) and the use of herbs and oils in magical spells, potions, and ointments. This comprises the third, or base, level of the three-tiered pantheon of the Asatru in both symbolism and reality, for it is the basic beginnings of what has come to be known as the Northern tradition. Even the mythological pattern makes it clear that it is the Lady who teaches natural magic to Odin, while the Runic magic of Odin is one obtained through self-sacrifice on the World-Tree, Yggdrasill. In the Tantric form of Aryan Hinduism, it is also the Goddess who teaches the gestures, symbolic markings, and lore that do not exist in the purely Aryan form of practice. Green Wicca is seen today more as the Anglo-Saxon version of the base level of the Northern tradition, the "Hedge Witch" of Great Britain as it were, with the deities derived from the Celtic, Gaelic, Pictish, and Anglo-Saxon heritage.

The practice of Green Wicca varies with the practitioner, as it tends to be utilized most often by the solitary witch, but includes the use of herbs in spells, some degree of shamanistic union with the energy through meditation, visualization, and even a variety of Tantric sexuality. This is not to say that *all* Green Witches utilize all these elements; rather, they tend to favor one or more of these approaches. There are many Wiccans who practice "Natural Wicca" and do not even consider themselves to be Green Witches, yet they use many of the Green techniques. While the term is not seen very often, the components of Green Witchcraft are used frequently by those called "traditional" or "family heritage" Witches.

The cross-fertilization of the earlier, universal beliefs and deities with those of the far-ranging Aryan conquerors results in a kind of deja vu sensation as Teutonic Pagan motifs appear in the modern mainstream religions of the Western world through the Near East. The tree from Eden, the sexuality of Eve, the crucifixion of God (Jesus) as a sacrifice to Himself (as Father)—all of these elements are Northern tradition carried into the Near East, assimilated, and brought back to Europe as a "new" religion. Part of the reason why the Germanic tribes could accept the new religion so quickly was because it mirrored their own Pagan beliefs—indeed, it *was* their faith.

The interconnectedness of religions is never so clear as when one considers the context of the Aryan religion merged with the first religion of humankind—that of the Goddess and the God. This took place in Northern Europe as a result of the natural evolution of human society, and in the Near East as the result of conquest, but the religion of the Indus was not erasable simply because it was the same as the "old" religion of the pre-Aryan Northern Pagans. To find out where the connections occurred, one must first follow the rise of the Aryan social structure and its effect on the religious practices of the Northern people. This is where it becomes obvious that the people of the South were not all that different from the people of the North—the Sun people, the Ice people—the Fire and Ice of the Teutonic tradition seen not as metaphor of the interaction of the cosmic forces that brings the universe into being, but as descriptive of the two sides of the same religion.

The main Teutonic deities may be categorized as Aesir and Vanir. The Aesir represent the deities of consciousness, law, and social order. This is the home realm of Odin (Woden), who is chief among the gods and goddesses of the Teutonic pantheon. His wife, Frigga, is a hearth deity concerned with things related to domesticity and the home—a woman's deity in a male-dominant hierarchy. But this is not the total picture. The Vanir are also very powerful deities, with the chief among them being the twins, Frey and Freya—the God and the Goddess of prehistoric and pre-Aryan times—and of the two, it is the Lady whose power allows Her to travel to Aesir at will. It is the Goddess who controls the cycles of Nature, has the power of magic (called seidh, or seith—which sounds rather like the Fairies

**Symbol of
Indra's
Thunderbolt**

or Sidhe—and therefore, the words used by the Dravidians), and uses natural substances in the practice of magic, including sexual activity (as is done in the Eastern Tantric practice). Here then, in the Vanir, is where East meets West, where Fire and Ice created the religious basis for both worlds in pre-Aryan times. But now there must be one more realm added to the hierarchy, and that is represented in Thor—the Thunderer—who is the God of the Warrior

Class. In Hinduism, he may be recognized as Indra, the Great Warrior of the Vedic (Aryan) rulers.

At the earliest stage of development, the Northern tradition was the same as the Southern tradition. But something happened to change that. In the South—in the Indus of 30,000 B.C.E.—a communal civilization arose, with no temples, no organized clergy, and no central authority. The practice of religion was a solitary tradition with the community gathering for celebrations of fertility, solstices, equinoxes, moon phases, and agricultural stages. The Northern tradition also began in this same manner. But the Northern climate and the land did not lend itself to the communal life-style of the Indus, and as society developed, villages grew, and population expanded, there arose leaders among the communities to guide and direct the life of the people. These chiefs needed to have others to aid in the protection of the community and to ensure their own rulership, and thus developed a warrior class to serve the rulers. The common people worshiped the God and the Goddess and knew the rituals and the magics of nature—they were Green Witches—and if the rulers kept to the same egalitarian deities, there would be nothing to sanctify their authority or set them apart from those they ruled. This could lead to challenges of authority and prevent a ruler from unifying his forces. With the advent of superior weaponry and battle skills came the birth of the Aryan conqueror. Frey was considered too gentle a God for a tribal chief, and in a time when strength of arms meant survival, Freya was not seen as representative of masculine prowess. In time, Frey would become the archetype for the gentle aspect of the Jesus of neighborly love, and Freya for the Mother of God, with both being submissive to the Father God.

Initially, the chiefs were nothing like the kings of Christian European history. Their warriors were farmers and herders of cattle who carried weapons for their chief when defense of the community was needed, or when expansion of territory was required. Durant states that the very word for "war" in the Aryan language simply translates into "a desire for more cattle." Able-bodied women were often part of the warrior class until marriage; then they were restricted by the duties of hearth and family. It would be centuries before this system would be altered into a "divine right" of kings and a warrior class who ruled serfs tied to the land they farmed for their overlord. Yet it was from the need for legitimacy in rulership that the need for a new God came—Odin, the God of Social Order; the God of a new magic called Runes, practiced by a select group, a nobility of rulers and warriors. The warriors who defended the community also needed a deity to bless them and set them apart from the farmers who were the Green Witches of the Vanir, and they received Thor, the Warrior God. It was in the religious practices that the change from equality between the sexes, and possibly a matriarchal power structure, shifted into male dominance, involving a male clergy who alone knew and transmitted the specialized rites of sacrifice to the deities associated with that particular class of people who now governed society.

It must have been a shock for the migrating Aryan conquerors to run into the expression and practice of Vanir religion again and again as they moved southward during their expansions, for this extolling of the way of the wise by Southern peoples was equally a

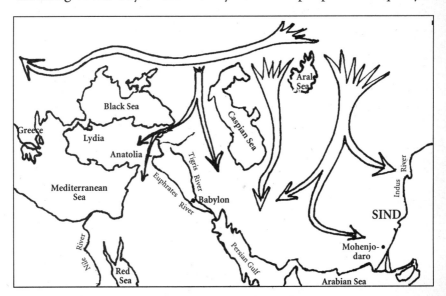

Aryan Migrations

glorification of the individualistic farmer/defender and a threat to the new Gods and powers of the Aryan warrior class. The one crucial difference between the fighting skill of the Aryans and that of the Indus people was in the forging of superior weapons, first of hardened bronze, then of iron. The Aryans had learned to use horse-drawn chariots in a way that gave the warrior strength, speed, and agility unmatched by the Southern peoples.

Iron was itself a secret kept by the Aryans for several centuries and was the primary source of their power. Durant shows that the Hittite Aryans used iron and their chariots to conquer the land between the Tigris and Euphrates Rivers, circa 1925–1800 B.C.E., and it was not until four centuries later that their contemporaries gained the knowledge. Soon after that, the Hittites disappeared from history. The knowledge of iron-making was a family tradition passed down from father to son for generations. It is no coincidence that the Fairies have a natural aversion to iron, for it was iron that destroyed their idyllic world.

Both Danielou and René Guénon, in *Fundamental Symbols of the Sacred Science,* consider the notion of civilization coming from the Aryans to be a myth that still affects modern research. They note that the Dravidic language is related to the Finnish, Hungarian, Turkish, Mongolian, and Eskimo languages, which is further evidence of the widespread nature of Dravidic contacts. It is their view that the Dravidians spread their culture to these areas before the Aryan invasions, during the Paleolithic Age prior to 20,000 B.C.E. when the first cave paintings were appearing in Europe. But aside from language and cultural similarities, no hard archaeological evidence has yet been uncovered to make the connection a historical fact—it is still theory, but theory that has wide acceptability.

The survivors of the Indus invasions (which began around 2150 B.C.E. and continued in stages until the destruction of Mohenjo-daro, circa 1200 B.C.E.) moved across the lands now known as Afghanistan, Iran, Iraq, Arabia, Palestine, Turkey, and through Eastern Europe into Western Europe. Their migrations are known to have gone as far as Indonesia, and, as previously considered, possibly into Japan, Polynesia, and as far as the Americas. They knew about boats, were active traders, and so they migrated away from the Aryan invaders and took their religion with them. For those moving into Europe, their religion was easily merged with that of the local populace: the veneration of the God and the Goddess, the celebration of the cycles of nature and fertility, and solitary practice were already local Pagan features.

The people of Sind (perhaps the source for the "Sindar" elves

Shiva Mahayogi (Great Teacher)

of Tolkien, who was an avid student and teacher of mythology and religions) were assimilated along with their language, giving birth to the Indo-European people and languages. Continuing waves of invasions in the Indus Valley resulted in waves of migrations, so that in time, the Dravidians were battling Indo-Europeans—people of their own heritage—for possession of places like Ireland, winning for a time, and then being displaced by later waves. This is the history of the Fir Bolgs, the Tuatha de Danu, and the Celts in Ireland, Wales, and Scotland. These are the Picts and these are the Fairie Folk. All represent the varying degrees of integration between the indigenous European population and the successive migrations of Dravidians.

Danielou and R. F. Willets agree that the people of Crete were most likely Dravidians, and note that the name Pandion, connected with the Sun and the Moon in festivals, relates to a tribe in Attica named Pandionis, and to the Dravidian dynasty Pandia— people who are recorded in the epic poem "Shilappadikaram" as fighting against the Aryans in the Mahabharata War, circa 1400 B.C.E. The Pandia tribal myth alleges that they descended from the Moon, and the name Pandu, whose sons fought the Aryan invaders, means "white."

Moving further westward were the Celts, whose origins are accepted by Danielou, Gwenc'hlan Le Scouezec, Anne Ross, and others as coming from the Indus Valley people. They traveled from the Iberian Peninsula northward, and by the seventh century B.C.E., their ithyphallic deity could be found carved in rock in Sweden and represented in wood in Denmark. This new influx of Indus people served to renew the Green Wicca traditions and preserve the Old Religion operating parallel to the Aryan system in a subordinate position, to later resurface as Teutonic Paganism.

The original primacy of the Old Religion, Witchcraft, over that of the patriarchal system of Odin and Thor is still evident in the mythology of the Northern Tradition. Freya, like Hecate, is the Goddess of eroticism and natural magic and is controller of the cycles of nature, and it is She who teaches Odin Her magic, to which is added His Runic magic. Yet She also knows this magic, and Runes are commonly used by Witches today. The consort of Freya is (in the familiar manner of many other Pagan systems) Her twin brother, and from these two come the Sun God and Moon Goddess, the twins Apollo and Diana, for example. This was easily accepted by Dravidian immigrants as manifestations of the united (twinned) Shiva/Shakti—the Horned God (since the God of the Northern tradition also represented eroticism, well-being, and the World) and the Goddess of Power.

The roots for the Wiccan and Pagan interchangeability of the aspects of the God and the Goddess comes from the integration of the traditions of Europe and Sind in the androgyne aspect of the Divine. Earth God, Earth Goddess; Sky God, Sky Goddess; God of Sea, Goddess of Sea; Lord of Beasts, Lady of Beasts; God of Fertility, Goddess of Fertility—these are all cross-identifications of Europe and Sind occurring over a period of a thousand years, from 2150 B.C.E. to 1200 B.C.E. This practice of the ancient and common tradition was relegated to the nonruling classes for the most part—it became the religion of the common people, the *paganus*, or "peasants." The higher godform of a ruling, father deity was politically created primarily to sanctify the earthly reality. Thus it is that the Vanir were the true foundation of the Northern tradition upon which was built that of the Aesir in the early days of Aryan migration and conquest. It is the pyramid of tradition, from Vanir to Aesir, with the younger, narrower tradition seated upon the base of the elder religion, but it is also the pyramid inverted to its point in terms of importance by the historical development of a few powerful rulers controlling the larger population.

Today, Northern Paganism is a vital mixture of the whole belief system. Although sometimes accused of racism and ties to Nazism, the tradition does not really encompass either of these. While a nationalistic interpretation was perverted by Hitler into a policy of racism, it was his aim to subvert Teutonic Paganism to serve his own ends. His archaeological efforts, however, did not lend support to his thesis of the Aryans being the conveyors of civilization. This line of investigation not only failed to support his claims of Aryan superiority, but went so far as to undermine it by showing that the Aryans had destroyed superior cultures. By then Hitler himself, seeing defeat in war coming, evoked this destructive image of the Aryans as a reflection of his own activities. The modern Northern tradition, however, claims to speak to a sense of association by heritage, but particularly in America, the usual norm of common language, as expressed by Thorsson (perhaps unintentionally), means that anyone who speaks English is a candidate for the Anglo-Saxon branch of Northern practice—which in America could then be a person of Italian, German, Polish, Scandinavian, Oriental, or African heritage by "blood," because, by the second and third generation, most of these ethnic groups are raised speaking English. If this is accepted, then the power of amalgamation in America could be one factor in making for a revitalization of Neo-Paganism, even a Northern tradition, without the racism remembered from the corruption initiated in Nazi Germany.

Wicca and the primal Vanir aspect of Teutonic Paganism are two versions of the same religious/magical system, with only the development of Runic magic (popularly used by both branches today, even if only for inscriptions and spell work) and the names given for the God and the Goddess being different. The incorporation of the Father God, Odin; Lawgiver, Tyr; and Warrior God, Thor, are indicative of the rise of law, rulership, and class distinctions in an early fighting society, spreading out into the civilized lands of Bronze Age cultures. Since modern societies still rely on laws for the governance of the population, and rulers (elected or otherwise) to direct the nations of the world, there is relevancy in the Asatru tradition. The fact that Americans and many other national peoples prefer a separation of church and state means that the expression of the Northern tradition is no longer reserved for those who rule, and can no longer be used as a means of authorizing that rule. The Father God and Warrior God may, therefore, be seen as superfluous by traditional Witches who follow the Green Path.

The Development of Ceremonial Magic: Its Relation to Wicca

In the Neo-Pagan community there are sometimes disagreements and controversies over which path is the most appropriate and valid. There is a traditional (and generally friendly) rivalry between Wiccans and ceremonial magicians (or mages) concerning magic in the terms of "high" and "low." Yet both groups recognize that "low magic" refers to material things. This can then be subdivided into creative (or white) magic and destructive (or black) magic. "High magic" is accepted by both groups as applying to the unifying of spirit and matter apart from either creative or destructive magic, and, therefore, transcendent rather than a practice of white or black magic. With Wicca the term "low magic" applies to the actual magical workings, as it does to ceremonialists, and "high magic" is the internal process affecting an individual at Esbats and Sabbats—celebrations usually ignored by ceremonialists. The controversy, then, stems from methodology and purpose, or attitude.

The ceremonialists got their most recent impetus with the formation of the Hermetic Order of the Golden Dawn in 1877 by three Masons in London. These men were influenced by the Enochian system created by Dr. John Dee, who was Queen Elizabeth's court astrologer in the sixteenth century, C.E. Members of the Golden Dawn later included Aleister Crowley (who left to form his own order—the Silver Star) and Dion Fortune in the twentieth century,

Great Vast Luck Scepter Charm
The writing of formulas in the magic circle familiar to ceremonial magic can be traced to the Tantric charms with written mantras.

and these two people did much to popularize the Order. Crowley (1875–1947) was a prolific writer, and much of his work continues to influence mages. His practices and teachings, those of the Golden Dawn, and the widely used Tarot of the Golden Dawn Order (Rider-Waite) incorporate the Hebrew kabbalah and letter symbology along with pre-Hebraic symbols of the Tree of Life, elements, Moon/Sun phases, Egyptian aspects (Book of Thoth), and even a touch of Hinduism (only the names of the Chakras and Kundalini are changed). Many Witches feel free to disregard the kabbalah aspects in their use of the Tarot for divination, and there are several Tarot decks available that are specifically designed for Wiccans.

It was Gerald B. Gardner (1884–1964) who, after spending many years of his life in the Shivan area of Sri Lanka and the Far East, popularized Wicca in the twentieth century. He wrote a number of books after "going public," once England's laws against Witchcraft were repealed in 1951. He claimed to have been initiated in 1939 and encouraged covens to meet "skyclad" (nude). This can be traced to Charles Leland's book, *Aradia* (1897), in which the practitioner was enjoined (in the "Charge of the Goddess") to be skyclad as a sign of being "really free," which indicates a lack of continuity in the understanding of the meaning of being clad in the sky. However, the Charge could also be a reference to the use of nakedness in India among devotees of Shiva as a sign of holiness and truth through virtue and freedom. Ritual nakedness, too, was symbolic among the Celts. Some Gardnerian covens tend to feel that Solitary Practitioners are not true Wiccans in that the Solitaries do not use degrees (from one of initiation to that of high priest/priestess). This is merely a point of artificial elitism against a Solitary tradition that has its roots in an earlier matriarchal descent—the "Grandmother" heritage that is sometimes disputed by organized coven traditions (such as the Seax-Wica denomination of Gardnerian Wicca created by Raymond Buckland in 1973, which recognizes Solitaries as authentic, but hereditary Witches as unlikely), although acknowledged by Gardner.

The Solitary Witches tend to be female and have a tradition of intuitive powers and the ability to function as "Natural Wiccans" passed down from mother to daughter, but often the present generation can only recall little more than two or three generations, and from this comes the expression. Yet the tendency of organized covens toward an orthodoxy and subsequent diminishing of the maternal inheritance has caused many female Solitary Wiccans to either remain silent to avoid debate or to begin to doubt their heritage. It is worth looking at the context of Gardner and Leland for an understanding of this question of recognized validity, although today, fortunately, there are few Wiccans who do not accept the reality of practicing Solitary Witches.

The Golden Dawn, Crowley, Leland (and later, to some degree, Gardner, who appears to have borrowed rituals from Leland and the Golden Dawn, in which order he was once an initiate, according to Aidan A. Kelly in his work, *Crafting the Art of Magic*), all came from a time when the social atmosphere of the Victorian Age (which did not end until 1901) was suffocating and impossibly strict. The Industrial Revolution had made a shambles of country life and family life; women were reduced in status even more than ever before in England—becoming pretty props for the male-dominated society, producing children and demurely running the household as the icons of morality and virtue, but incapable of serious thought. The dark and depressing aspects of life in the Victorian Age almost never seem to make it to the pretty films about that time period. The ugly side of balls and flouncy dresses, big houses, elegant living, and lots of servants is carefully ignored, even in modern movies and stories, unless it is a film dealing specifically with the downside of the period. The whole vision rarely appears, and instead, people grow up today remembering Shirley Temple as the "Little Princess," the lavish classical films of life in the Victorian Era, and costume affairs based on Charles Dickens novels.

The horrible fact is that women were often given clitorectomies at an early age (twelve thru fourteen being most popular) so that they would not be able to enjoy sexual relations. If they became "rebellious" due to the lack of purpose in their confined lives, they were sent to hospitals for hysterectomies to remove their uteruses. Anesthetic in the form of ether had just been discovered, and it would appear that doctors were eager to use it as often as possible. Nevertheless, this use of cruel and unnecessary debilitating surgery is reminiscent of Nazi surgeries on concentration camp prisoners. It is hard to imagine the trauma and fear that would be instilled in a young girl who had been so brutally maimed or in an adult woman so casually violated.

Women went from the "protection" of their fathers or brothers to the "protection" of their husbands. They could not legally own property, they could not buy or sell anything without a man's approval, and they were certainly not expected to take part in any intelligent conversation with males—obedience and submission was their lot in life. For the lower classes of workers and domestics, the rules were the same, but impossible to uphold due to the working status of many women. Thus lower-class women were frequently exploited shamefully by men of all classes, with nowhere to turn for relief, and they often ended up as prostitutes or wet nurses to support their fatherless children.

If any woman became too difficult to control, she could be medically sedated and tranquilized, locked in a room for days, weeks, or months until her protector decided she had regained self-control; forced into a surgery promoted by the male medical profession as a means of controlling hysteria (hence the term hysterectomy); or she could be declared insane by a male protector (either family member or one arbitrarily assigned by the legal system) and sent to an insane asylum, where male doctors could, in the tradition of Freud, then expound upon the sexually based psychological problems of women. This then is the environment at the beginnings of modern ceremonial magic and Leland's Wicca.

The quaint displays of sexual freedom in an inhibited time come from a restricted and naive people who were titillated by coven gatherings where a man might actually touch a female's private parts, as when the priest (even the covens were male dominated, with the Priestess taking her cues from the Priest) anointed women on their breasts and genitals, and then had the satisfaction of being anointed in turn by a woman. The advent of secret societies, occultism, and seances popular at this time was a reaction against Victorian social strictures, and included some rather childish antics designed to be "outrageous." Crowley was a master showman who enjoyed shocking polite society with his flamboyant displays of iconoclastic abandon, as when he painted the numbers 666 on his forehead and named himself "The Beast." Modern Fundamentalist Christians would today be as horrified as the religious people of the nineteenth century.

All this really shows, superficially, is a desire to throw off the bonds of convention, but underneath is something much more enduring and ancient, something that was finally and properly released when two world wars turned the artificial social order upside down. The Old Religion was not dead, and in the wake of new freedoms and an increasing equality of the sexes brought about by the need of men and women to fight in unison for their mutual survival, the suppressed Old Ways—the Vanir traditions of the common people—were brought out into the light.

Thus, while initially the modern advent of occultism, magic, and skyclad covens may have been an attempt to renounce the stifling effects of the Victorian Age, and doubtless this feature did lure a number of people to learn about Wicca, the fact remains that there is historical evidence that some ancient peoples did perform rituals naked, and included sexual intercourse as part of the process. This is especially easy to see in Etruscan funeral cave paintings (Massa and others show these), where men and women are depicted copulating between the furrows of freshly plowed fields. Yet this same act is depicted in Christian-inspired artwork as naked female Witches copulating with demons from hell and eating children. It is all a matter of context in the historical sense, and a blending in the Christian mind of Pagan rites with anti-Christian rites. The two do not belong together, as the first is religious expression, and the second is a protest against a particular religion.

It took a little while for the people experimenting with a revival of Pagan practices to realize that what they were doing was not "exciting" so much as it was energizing—channeling the Universal Energy focused through the elements and the God and the Goddess directly into their bodies to be used for whatever purpose they desired. People were finally able to cast aside the artificial inhibitions of the Judeo-Christian tradition and recognize that their sexuality was nothing to be ashamed of; that the human body was not ugly or evil; that sexual behavior was not a sin. Although humankind may no longer feel it necessary to perform sexual rites in the fields to ensure a good crop, people may now enjoy the energy and joy of sexual pleasure without fear or guilt. Education and knowledge make all the difference.

To the Craft, magic is a natural phenomenon involving the cosmic energy of the elements of Nature. Focusing may be achieved through rituals that vary from elaborate to simple, to effect the tuning in with natural forces for accomplishing a desired result. To the ceremonialist, magic is achieved by the mage controlling the forces of nature by controlling what he *perceives* as the divine. Both methods work because both provide a means for aligning one's own energies with existing external energies for redirection. The reason a person chooses to be a Witch or a mage is based upon personal preference, personality, and sometimes simply what was readily available when first starting out to work magic. Mages, such as Kenneth Deigh in his article "Clearing the Air" (*The Llewellyn New Times*, Number 915, Sep/Oct 1991), sometimes even state as their reason the desire to display their power to subvert the divine to their own will. This is different from the Wiccan concept of joining with the divine to work to an end (not a surrendering of the self to the Deity, as Deigh has perhaps properly defined general religion, but improperly defined Witchcraft and the Wiccan religion). Ceremonialism is instead an attempt to dominate the forces in order to redirect them through internalizing the force of energy and then sending it back out.

Whereas the Witch unites with the energy, the ceremonialist attempts to be superior to it, and therefore can never aspire to complete satisfaction because of the impossibility of the task he sets for himself. The mage tries to absorb the All into the Self, but the Self cannot contain the All—this would be self-destructive—and yet this is the ceremonialist's ideal. Not even an adept can hope to conquer the divine, for that would mean to replace the divine in power, and therein lies egotism that would surely make Shiva smile. One can be god, but not the God; one can be divine, but not the Divine, and this inbuilt restriction can pose a problem for the ceremonialist in conducting effective magic.

The main difficulty with ceremonial magic comes from its basis in the Hebrew kabbalah. The Hebrew religion is itself the product of Aryan Levites attempting to eradicate an older religious system, and only dates back to around 621 B.C.E. as the start of an orthodox form, while the Israelite people themselves can be placed at circa 1250 B.C.E. The kabbalah can be traced to the Renaissance with German magicians and to Dr. John Dee in England. The current ceremonial tradition most widely recognized, the Golden Dawn, incorporates both Dee's Enochian system and the kabbalah. Gershom Scholem, in his *Origins of the Kabbalah*, shows that some aspects of the kabbalah system were known in Provence, France, around 1130 C.E., but felt these were based on earlier, separate sources. The oldest known manuscript is dated to 1298 C.E. and was translated into Latin for Flavius Mithridates and used by Mirandola in 1486 C.E. So basically, despite allegations of the ancient origins of

Mystic Monogram
The monogram is composed of ancient Indian seed syllables crowned by the crescent moon and sun, arranged in a manner reminiscent of Egypt.

the kabbalah, the historic reality is in the Jewish community of Medieval Europe.

Curiously enough, Scholem admits that there are elements in the Kabbalah that do not reflect the traditions of Medieval Jews. Instead, he alludes to unknown influences stemming from an earlier time in Italy and from the Orient, which is not surprising since the Hindu missionaries were well-established in Rome and throughout the Empire. The kabbalistic use of Hebrew letters to perform magic can be traced to the mysticism of Hinduism and the Buddhist interpretation originally intended to regain the power of the priest class. The fifty letters of the Hindu alphabet are said to constitute the body of the Goddess in the Tantric tradition, and by placing the letters on different parts of a person's body, the mortal body can be transformed into a divine one, limb by limb. Constant chanting of mantras accompanies the writing process, which is considered to work because Shakti is matter (while Shiva is spirit). The use of circles with sacred letters and symbols used by the ceremonialist is reminiscent of the Hindu mandala ("circle").

In addition, it is now accepted that the Hebrews were never an outside people who entered into Canaan with a different ethnic and religious background, but were themselves Canaanites who wandered as they tended flocks, while other Canaanites dwelled in cities where they made goods and raised crops in nearby fields that would in turn support the herders. The distinctions between the herders and the farmers were based on occupation and dwelling place, not ethnic or religious background. Here was a society of one people interacting for mutual benefit in a division of labor. It is known that after 1250 B.C.E. there was a combination of political, climatic, and economic factors in the Mycenean kingdoms of the Aegean that affected the entire Mediterranean world. This correlates with the final conquest of the cities of the Indus Valley as well, and so it becomes clear that the Aryans were again pushing southward in a wave of conquest and destruction.

The disruption of trade and political upsets resulted in the Canaanite cities being abandoned decades before the supposed "conquest" of the Canaanites by Joshua in the Bible stories. Instead, there was a slow change whereby the wandering herders began to settle on hilltops to make up for the absence of support from the cities in the valley. Thus, with refugees from the cities, the hilltops were turned into more defendable settlements where land would be cleared and crops planted, while the herders now had community goods available closer to their flocks. Archaeologists have concluded that the stories of Exodus and Joshua were created by court poets eager to flatter the later Israelite and Judean kings. The slavery of the

Doré's depiction of the Egyptians drowning in the Red Sea.

Jews in Egypt and the "Passover" never happened, but are merely the contrivance of the Aryan Levites, with borrowings from Assyrian myths, to explain the Pagan celebration of the Spring Equinox in a way that made it acceptable to the Aryan religion.

Danielou points out that this type of writing, wherein history is used to promote a cause while distorting reality, has been used many times, and gives Livy's *History* as an example. Livy's diatribes against the Dionysian cults—an attempt at discrediting them by claiming they were guilty of such crimes as incest, killing and eating newborn babies, and drinking blood—were not based on actual practices but upon a campaign of slander. It has taken archaeology to point the way to the truth. The allegations of Livy are echoed in the Christian allegations of Witchcraft activities and are equally false. Indeed, these charges of baby-eating have been leveled against a designated opposition in order to unite people against an enemy throughout European and American history. The latest examples include World Wars I and II, where the English and the Germans made the accusation against each other, and the 1992 American Presidential campaign where Republican Christian Fundamentalist Pat Robertson claimed that the Equal Rights Amendment (supported by the Democrats) encouraged women to kill their babies, divorce their husbands, and become Witches and lesbians. In these ways are the distortions of history maintained to modern times.

The true history of the Israelites shows that the population in Canaan was local, and the Israelites were not nomads so much as they were pastoralists. It would compare to there being two types of people in Europe at the collapse of the Roman Empire in circa 476 C.E.—herders living in the open and farmers/craftsmen/traders living in cities, tending nearby fields, and plying their crafts. Trade collapses when the empire falls, the cities are deserted, and the population gravitates outward. The herders eventually make more permanent settlements to grow food and create shelter, and soon there are castles with a warrior class for protection and fiefs with serfs to maintain the system. The serfs, then, are the Hebrews, and the Aryan Levites are the overlords, and from these latter people come the princes and kings of Israel and Judea. The Israelites were the refugees of Canaan, and the Aryan Levites were the conquerors.

Then what does this do to ceremonial magic and its reliance on the Hebrew kabbalah? Since the main characters of the Bible were not real, it is useless to believe that there was a "Key of Solomon." Everything in the Bible, besides being relatively recent, is borrowed from a variety of older non-Hebrew sources and altered to promote Judaism and the domination of the Hebrew people by their Levite overlords. This was a deliberate effort, rather than an example of cultural evolution, and the same technique was used by the Roman Catholic Church in its early centuries to gain a position of power when the Roman Empire began its gradual collapse.

The Church had rival texts burned (as many as 10,000 books in one day in one city, John Romer reports) and closed all the schools and institutions of higher learning (of which there were many in the Roman world). Danielou laments that the Church burned libraries and destroyed monuments. Professors were killed along with students and all identifiable dissenters, and a strict orthodoxy was imposed in which violators would be executed. The same tactics were used by Stalin to control the diverse people of the U.S.S.R. In the newly Christianized Europe, the only people who could speak to God on behalf of the common folk and who had the ability to read the Sacred Text were the priesthood, consisting only of males—women were not educated, and those whose male relatives were kind enough to get them tutors could not advance in the Church's power system, but had to rely on blessings and sacraments from the priests.

The Church was not the "repository" of education in the Dark Ages, but the *cause* of ignorance and illiteracy, while the power inherent with knowledge was a coveted possession of the Church hierarchy. The Church *created* the Dark Ages, then created the schools and system of education that followed to promote the Church in heroic terms. The Spanish conquistadors described the Aztec City of Mexico as the most beautiful in the world, but following the lead of the Church, they destroyed it all, burned the libraries, and wiped out a heritage that surpassed their own. In Europe after Constantine, any divergence from Church doctrine was met with the cry of heresy, and that could lead to torture and brutal death. It has taken the Roman Catholic Church, that alleged savior of education, until nearly the close of the twentieth century to at last *consider* agreeing with Gallileo.

It was not until the twelfth century Renaissance that education began to reappear in Europe, although it was in the hands of the Church and carefully supervised to agree with Church doctrine. The tenuous steps of scholasticism typify the atmosphere that produced the kabbalah. So who are the "Names of Power," divine personages, Olympic spirits, angels, demons, archangels, arch-demons and so forth of the ceremonialist's kabbalah? They are the Pagan Gods and Goddesses being displaced and restructured—often with a sex change to remove females from positions of power—by the comparatively new religion of the Aryan Levites. To practice rites based on the Kabbalah is to accept the rather late-coming religion of the Hebrews as an authoritative source. In the twelfth and sixteenth centuries this was a natural thing to do, since the Catholic Church directed religious thought in the Western world until the beginnings of sixteenth century Protestantism, but all Christian denominations still accepted the Bible as historical truth. Knowing now that this is false, the kabbalah becomes less credible and less valuable as a tool for combining with the natural energies of the Earth and the Universe. It also makes Witchcraft and the Vanir level of Teutonic Neo-Pagan traditions stronger by comparison as it is their Ancient Ones who have been renamed and cataloged in the Kabbalah.

This need for acceptance of Judaism as an authoritative distillation of what predates it, rather than as the new religion of its time, attempting to obliterate all that had come before, requires one to put aside knowledge in order to work within the system. The ceremonialist, then, becomes an inadvertent supporter of Judaism and all the religions that have sprung from that source, rather than a representative of an older, historic Pagan tradition. The Wiccan does not have to deal with this problem since invocations do not involve a lengthy appeal to Jewish ethereal spirits who are not reliably what they are supposed to be, anyway. Renaissance mages were floundering in a sea of misinformation, but they could put it together in a way that worked for them because they did not know that they were ignorant. Today this system is made harder to work with because one must deliberately suspend one's understanding of the historical truths of the Hebrew people and Judaism to make it function. In Wicca, no "Names of Power" are needed; no "letters of power" (not to be confused with Runes) are necessary.

Even if the kabbalah is not the Renaissance invention (based, as it were, on scraps of Medieval Jewish Gnostic material) many historians believe it to be, and its tradition reverts to an older Hebrew source, it is still a compromised attempt to hold onto the pre-Judaic traditions of magic in nature. Scholem does not deny that the sources may go back into antiquity, but historians and archaeologists know today that Judaism does not. Danielou notes that one effect of Jewish monotheism was to distance them from the more ancient cosmological traditions, so it is very likely that some Jews sought to preserve this information in a socially and politically acceptable manner. Unfortunately, the side effect was to lose the purity of natural magical practices and to infuse a taint of racism, intolerance, and egotism (having the only "correct" God and being "chosen") that has persisted to this day in Jewish orthodox faith and in many of the denominations of its Christian and Islamic descendants. Prior to this, the Gods and Goddesses of other cultures were accepted and were even incorporated into the local pantheons.

Return to a time before the Hebraic rituals, or the overworked intricacies of the Egyptian priesthood, and the original basis of both ceremonial and craft magic is clear—all rests upon the flow of the Eternal Energy, that spark of life that exists in all living things and cannot be destroyed, but is immortal and thus makes life itself immortal; the unity and the separateness of male and female; the elements; Sun phases; Moon phases; seasonal changes; and the natural schedules for planting and harvesting. Bulls and snakes come into use as the ancient symbols of strength, fertility, wisdom, and

**Egyptian Priest offering a Libation and an Oblation,
Precursor to the Modern Eucharist**

rebirth; trees as symbols of knowledge and truth (from which the word is derived) from which comes the understanding of life.

The point that is frequently repeated in Neo-Pagan gatherings and conversations between traditions is that there really is no "right" way, only paths that have worked for different people in different times—ways that others adopt for themselves in order to find direction, or at least a starting point. Today there are many books openly available that deal with spells, rituals, magic techniques, and divination methods. Practitioners of the Craft may be skyclad, robed, or dressed in any way that feels right to the individual, whether as a group (coven) decision or as a solitary. One may draw the symbols and call upon the spirits of ceremonial magic and still feel contact with the power of the natural energies, just as the mainstream religionists may tap into that same energy when in fervent prayer. But the problem with the kind of diversity prevalent in Neo-Paganism, as Danielou sees it, is the inherent loss of direction and isolation due to an approach that is often restricted through lack of knowledge and reduced to an almost continuous improvisation (as seen in the writings of Starhawk). This is a view that leads some Neo-Pagans to suggest an orthodoxy might be in order to concentrate the efforts of the practitioners. Most Neo-Pagans, however, are sufficiently independent to reject this or any other type of regimentation. The seeker must therefore be sincere and persistent in order to gain understanding, yet alert and cautious to avoid being victimized by popular crazes and baseless initiations.

The principle of Karma remains in effect no matter what path is taken, and this is why even Christians are cautioned not to judge others lest they be judged, and to remember that vengeance is not to be meted out by the individual, but by God (as Karmic energy). If the negative aspects of the subconscious are dredged up to focus on "dark powers," the unpleasant results actually rebound upon the user, and this makes the use of "black" magic hazardous, not to the object of the magic, but to the practitioner. Gardner's Wiccan Rede of "An' it harm none, do as thou wilt," is matched in Christianity with "Do unto others as you would have them do unto you," and in the ancient Witchcraft injunction that what is sent out comes back (threefold, according to some traditions). The thrust of these redes is that people are discouraged from projecting negativity for their own sake.

The advantage of Neo-Paganism is the absence of the baggage of guilt and unworthiness so often heaped upon the mainstream believers. Humans as individuals need to relate to the environment and to that spark of Divinity that dances in all life as well as in each person, and there are many paths to choose from to achieve this goal. The acceptance of this one fact is what prevents orthodoxy from gaining a grip on Pagan practices. The validity of one system or another is moot, as all are as valid as their practitioner's ability to use them—whether they have a history centuries old, or are relatively new—because humans are not a stagnant species. As long as the mind and spirit function, progress can be made, and no religious system (not even the Judeo-Christian-Islamic systems as evidenced by the variety of denominations in each) can expect to freeze the human heart in mid-beat to adhere to one set of rituals or beliefs. The energy of the Neo-Pagan/Wiccan movement is in its flexibility and open acceptance of its continuing evolution. There will never be a "Mother Church" nor orthodoxy for Pagans, as it is the spirit of individuality that distinguishes modern Paganism from mainstream religions.

It is significant, however, that the structural needs of the ceremonialist system have crept into the Craft through the establishment of Wiccan "traditions" created by people with former associations with ceremonial orders like the Golden Dawn. This has resulted in a Wicca that does not genuinely reflect the "Old Religion" of Witchcraft. The Green Witch does not follow prescribed rituals, does not feel compelled to perform specific motions, and does not even require the accouterments so often associated with Witchcraft. Marian Green in her book, *A Witch Alone,* recognizes that Witchcraft is a religion without dogma, but there are still those whose practice of the Craft projects a patriarchal and rigid ritualistic point of view. For some seekers, such a tradition may be useful as a starting place, but for others it could be inhibiting or a drain on their personal power.

There are, in fact, people who are Witches who have never attended a coven, never followed a prescribed ritual, and have had such great success at their practice that they have been sought out for advice, spells, divinations, and healings. One does not become a Witch by following another's path, but by making the connection with the Lord and the Lady individually. This can be (and has been) done in the context of accepted religions. The Craftwise have worked through the centuries within the system, in some cases even as members of a nature tradition such as the Lay Order of Saint Francis, in the nations where the Catholic system has overlapped the Pagan. This is particularly evident in Central and South America, and in the Caribbean Islands, but can also be said of the Mediterranean nations and Eastern Europe. There has never been an Inquisition in Romania, for example, and Witches have never been consistently persecuted there.

The Alexandrian tradition created by Alex and Maxine Sanders is based on the rituals of the Gardnerian tradition, and Gardner's own rituals have been traced to the Golden Dawn (although many Gardnerians may argue the point). So whereas it can be supposed that the Neo-Pagan coven movement in Wiccan traditions has ties to ceremonial magic, the magical, herbal, and connective practices of the solitary (Green) Witch harken to Sind. The Seax (Saxon) Wicca tradition recently created by Raymond Buckland evolved from his Gardnerian background and dissatisfaction (and perhaps even as a joke, according to Adler). Over and over, the roots of these traditions revert to Gardner and the morass of ceremonialism. Such roots do not reflect the Old Religion of nature, but rather what Danielou sees as the relatively childish Western Judaic-based theological concepts whose dogma and tyranny does not provide the answers people are seeking.

This lack of satisfaction in religion has caused a veritable eruption of alternative religious styles in what has been labeled the New Age. The seeker, however, must always continue to learn and grow. The Aryan influence of form over content has permeated religious expression in the West for so long that it is difficult for people to recognize the Sind elements and return to the source of humanity's first religion. One can take as a clue, however, that when a ritual or ceremony becomes annoying or boring, as was the case with the initiation of a young woman (who herself appeared to be moved by the experience) into Alexandrian Wicca, as described by Adler, then one has moved away from the source.

When leaders of Wiccan traditions announce that theirs is the only true path, that initiations and degrees are required, and that ritual formulae and attire (or lack thereof) must be followed, they are inadvertently expressing a connection to ceremonialism. When the kabbalah is incorporated into the Wiccan structure, the ancient craft is compromised. Most writers on the subject will admit that many elements from ceremonial magic have entered into Witchcraft, but one need only remember that the magic comes from within, and that the trappings are incidental. The seeker must first identify what needs require filling, and search for the path that best meets those needs. Fear of questioning has no place in Neo-Paganism, and structures that deny this are self-serving and not much different from the mainstream religions.

"Perfect love and perfect trust" and going naked before the Divine does not necessarily refer to nudity, but rather to internal soul-baring, for there are no secrets from the God and the Goddess. The concept of using sexual energy to accomplish a goal is one fraught with dangers and may not be as successful as earth-raised energy through dancing and chanting, simply because sex is a normal activity—one to be celebrated and enjoyed, but with equality between the participants. It is this sense of equality that is missing from much of the Buddhist Tantric tradition. Buddhism, having begun as an Aryan reform movement in Hinduism, speaks to the dominant male aspect of the religion, and thus Danielou can write of Tibetan Buddhists using prostitutes in certain rituals, and of the male-oriented nature of the Vedic-Shivan sects, while yet acknowledging that the original Shivan people were matriarchal. The very practice of this type of sexual magic is then degrading to the women who make up half of the process. This is a flawed perspective of the union of Shiva and Shakti. The Goddess is not a prostitute; She is not used, then discarded. To do so with a woman is demeaning to the perfect union of the God and the Goddess, and demonstrates the influence of the Aryan, male-dominant, political deities.

The sexual aspect in a coven setting could devolve into a way of controlling people and giving them a sense of participation without actually providing any real information on how to work magic; and should disagreements take place among the members, the potential for trouble is greater. The seeker must always remain alert to the possible abuse of power in coven traditions. Magic comes from within, and is not a matter of initiation or pronouncement. Only the practitioner knows what he/she feels when working magic, and when one feels it work, someone else's initiation is irrelevant.

The evolution of a priesthood came from one group of people keeping secrets from the rest of the people so as to generate and hold power over them. Danielou, speaking from the viewpoint of Vedic Shivan tradition, considers the written word as invalid in magic, for the formulas need to be passed along orally. In Wicca there are some who believe that power shared is power lost, and so encourage secrecy. With the Catholic Church, the same tradition is applied to the portion of the mass wherein the consecration of the host and wine takes place, with these words mumbled under his breath by the priest so no one in the congregation knows what he is saying. Only an initiate—another priest—knows the magic formula. Then what about the numerous spell books available in bookstores? These are also not complete. For one to practice magic effectively, one must put part of oneself into the process. Scott Cunningham was most clear about this in his writings when he advised people to alter the spells and to add their own words.

There is more to Witchcraft than form and ritual. It is a craft—an art—and will therefore vary with the person practicing it. To say that one must be initiated by someone else who has been initiated and establish a lineage to Gardner is to ignore the fact that Witches come from all over the world, not just Great Britain. The source of Witchcraft travels with the Green Witch, the Celts, the Etruscans, the Gypsies, and the Indus Dravidians, back to Sind. In order to work magic effectively, one need only turn to the source, for as Marian Green explained it, the God and the Goddess will provide. Accepting this unconditionally is the true meaning of "perfect love and perfect trust."

Wicca needs to be more than the ceremony of the Sabbats. It is not reasonable to put aside knowledge (the very thing the God and Goddess want humanity to possess) in order to perform seasonal rites mourning the death of the God, honoring His rebirth at Winter Solstice, cheering Him on in His pursuit of the Goddess, acting as voyeurs at Their union, and honoring His entering the soil for the harvest, Her pregnancy, and so on through the cycle anew. People today should be aware that the seasons will change and the seeds will sprout whether people are here or not—that is the order of Nature. Then what are Witches supposed to be doing at the Sabbats? Are they practicing the rituals of a newly entrenched clergy to dominate others, or mimicking rituals once believed essential? The first is manipulative and the second is shallow. Over time, with education improving and becoming more commonplace, the old Judeo-Christian images become more quaint than realistic; the rituals are a form of social conduct; the extremism is blunted—that is why education is the bane of those organized religions that have maintained power through control of education. To fall into this same trap would be the end of Wicca.

Witchcraft can be little more than a variation of that same mainstream form unless it is allowed to evolve, as humanity evolves. To be effective, Wicca cannot remain fixated on a dimly remembered past. It is not a protest statement, but an intuitive understanding and union with Nature. Danielou notwithstanding, this cannot be legislated by ritual formats and by sculpted words, as Starhawk discovered in her book, *The Spiral Dance*. Intuition must be felt by anyone who would be called a Witch, and it is because of the personal nature of this intuition that a rigid tradition based upon a hierarchy of degrees of initiation is impossible. This is essentially a manifestation of an element of natural chaos disrupting the human-created law of the sect.

Play is the word often used to describe how a Witch makes contact with the All, but, as with children, even play must be rational on its own level and abide by its own rules of engagement. Thus the value of the solitary tradition lies in the fact that no energy need be lost or wasted trying to align a number of people's rules of engagement. In the practice of ceremonial magic, the use of terms and forms that were once the Pagan Gods and Goddesses, revised into demons and angels under an Aryan rulership, is actually an insult to the Lord and Lady. This, in itself, may be one reason why some people (such as Migene González-Wippler has herself experienced and discussed in her writings) report bizarre and self-injurious results from their attempts. Their subconscious is offended and directs the subsequent anger upon the conscious for the outrage of imposed ignorance. It is only after the subconscious is beaten into submission that ceremonialism can begin to appear effective. The inner awareness was trying to chastise the outer, not destroy it, so it becomes a weak voice where it could have been a strong one.

The rigid form of some Wiccan traditions requires the same sort of willful ignorance, and that is also an affront to the Tree of Knowledge. So what do the Sabbats and Esbats mean to the modern Witch? The Sabbats are calls to the elements, who are the kin of humanity and live within each person, and to the substance and energy that forms and animates the individual. It is a "homecoming" or "reunion" between one's conscious mind and awareness with the transcendental forces united through one's subconscious. When the Witch invokes (not "summons") the elements and the Deities, the Self is opened to flow freely with the larger aspect of what forms the individual. Danielou describes the God and the Goddess in Tantric cosmological terms, with Shiva being the primal explosive force which created the Universe, pushing the particles and energy away from the source, and Shakti being the force that brings the energy and particles together to form the stars and solar systems. These opposites are found in all of existence, and, just as it is the aim of the Shivaite to bring about the union of the opposites within the individual, so it is the goal of the Witch, whose religion can be traced back to Sind, to do the same.

With four of the Sabbats (Yule, Ostara, Litha, and Mabon), one may find that the Solstices and Equinoxes generate a natural desire within to join with the ebb and flow of energy and particles—like a planet drawn to a sun, the spirit yearns for union with the larger mass of cosmic energy at those times when the energies are at their greatest, equal, or weakest force. Perhaps there is a subconscious feeling that by opening the Self to the flow, one may draw the energy tides back and forth, as the sea tides are pulled by the Moon. Hence people worldwide, expressing this sensation through different forms and different religions, become the moons for the elements and the Deities, who participate in the unions as much as the celebrants.

Marking the Esbats brings people into alignment with their Moon essence and intuitive abilities, and thus affords the best results for doing magic. The Moon unites with one's personal tides, both internal and external. For the other four Sabbats, internal restoration and alignment are the focus. With Imbolc, the time is appropriate for cleansing, purifying the inner temple of the Self; a time for restoring one's balance, for rededication, or for performing an internal house-cleaning. Beltane is a time for feeling renewal and the joy of life in alignment with the Earth's springtime. Lughnasadh brings a feeling of comfort and plenty which can be appropriately celebrated with a bread festival to acknowledge the Earth's bounty with gratitude and respect. Samhain is the time when one's spirit reaches out to unem-bodied souls with the instinctive recognition that all are of the same essence, no matter what the outer form or place in the corporeal world. The sepulcher of Jesus is no more than another interpretation of the similar theme from Dionysus, whose temples contained a rep-resentation of the tomb. The God of life has traditionally been asso-ciated with the harvest and with death, to be like Hades, the God of the Underworld, or like Shiva, the King of Shadows. The aspect of the God as Time and Destroyer has its place in the darkness of the turning of the seasons. Now the Goddess moves alone as the Crone, devoid of Her Shiva, until the Winter Solstice renews Her as Mother with the rebirth of the God. But it is with Samhain that the Witch finds a quiet, somber mood in which to reflect upon the gentle union all beings hold together as spirits flowing from life to life through the passage called death, and to know that all are an integral and per-sonal part of this great fluctuation of energy through matter.

Danielou sees a trend emerging in the Western world to a return to the concepts of Shiva, but links the return to a respect for nature with the particularly male-focused practice of the sex magics of the Tantras. This is still a reflection of the Aryanization of the religion of Sind, for the Vedic Shivan practice still does not demon-strate the balance of the Lord and the Lady—Ardhanari. There are Tantric Shakti practices as well, but it is the legacy of Aryanism that has left this union split asunder.

(Top and Left) **Wiccan altar set with images of Sind for a Full Moon Esbat celebration—disk has a pentagram carved upon it.** (Bottom) **Pottery dishes used to hold the candles marking the quarters of the circle: N – Green, E – Yellow, S – Red, and W – Blue.**

With the Tantrics, evolved from the Puranas texts written between 900 and 1000 C.E., the message remains essentially the same as with the modern Fundamentalists of Judaic-Christian-Islamic traditions, namely that only those followers of the God will survive an apocalypse to create a new human race. Dravidic Shiva puts His hand to His forehead and shakes His head. This is not the message of Sind, it is not the message of the first worldwide religion of humanity, but the Aryan message of exclusivity and intolerance that has sullied human affairs in the Near East and Western worlds for 3,000 years.

If one can accept that one is part of the universal flow of energy through matter, then there is no apocalypse—for there is no "ending," only the continual ebb and flow of all life in energy. The tides of electrons and neutrons, of Moon and Earth, of Practitioners of any number of faiths and Sun phases, are but a microcosm of the tides of the Universe itself. Danielou makes much of the comparisons of ancient texts, but, as with Kersten, the link of one set of Aryan documents with another is not sufficiently established to show that similarity in these doctrines should be anticipated, and that they differ from what pre-dated them in Sind. It is the message of Shakti, as the Tree of Life—denied by the Aryan politicized religion—that all people are immortal, that is missing. Not only may the East help the West recover its lost traditions, as René Guénon suggests in *The Crisis of the Modern World,* but the West may help the East, in return, by reminding it that it has the politically exclusive elements of Western Aryanism intermixed in its ancient Hindu and associated religions. Together, Orient and Occident may yet find union in the application of a purer Sind tradition.

Hitler and the Holocaust

Much has been written about the six million Jews who were killed in the Nazi Holocaust during World War II, but what about the other six million people who were exterminated? What motivation did Hitler have for all of these deaths, and what led him to select his victims? Although people have known for many years that Hitler was very interested in the occult and sought a revival of Germanic Paganism to support his regime, this has generally been dismissed as only further evidence of his insanity. But as one studies the subject of religion and the spread of and "pollution" of the Aryan ideals, one can see the "method" to Hitler's "madness."

The other six million, as briefly delineated by Martin Gilbert in *The Holocaust: A History of the Jews of Europe During the Second World War*, are the real clue as to the purpose of the Holocaust. The Jews were not the first people to be targeted by the Nazi regime as the people who had to be erased in order to return to the Paganism of the Aryans. The "cleansing" first consisted of the mentally ill, Gypsies, Slavs, and homosexuals, because of what they represented from the historical, occult, and religious points of view. It was through Romania and Hungary that the early Celts had arrived in Eastern Europe and spread across what is modern Austria, Switzerland, and France. The Slavs, and the Gypsies who wandered across

Europe taking with them the early beliefs and customs of their ancient forebears, posed a threat to the new mythology of Aryan superiority being created by Hitler.

By tracing the history of religion, language, and civilization in an unbiased fashion, one discovers that the Near East was not the place of origin for the great ideas of humankind, but the later area that preserved these concepts for historical record. Much of the Hebrew written account and mythology in the Pentateuch revolves around the denial of the earlier systems of belief and the ostracism of those who retained any aspect of those beliefs. Because the record is available for anyone who reads, the Jewish people were targeted for extermination—as were Christians, but for them the extermination would progress after the other deaths had been accomplished. In time, the Catholic Church would have been a target, and so would have any Protestant religious group. A major result of a successful Holocaust would have been the institution of upper level Aryan Paganism *in its pure form*, without the lower (Green) level from which it had evolved.

The source of the "contamination" of Aryan Paganism (and subsequently of Judaism and its family offshoots) was the religion of the Indus Valley—the indestructible God and Goddess, Shiva and Shakti; AUM and UMA. The Jews had to be killed to destroy the record they had so faithfully kept without realizing the implications of what they were keeping. The Gypsies had to be killed because they were the original wanderers from India who kept the ancient faith in their own way. The Slavs had to be killed because they were the closest to the ancient people who migrated from India and retained many of the Indus traditions. The homosexuals had to be killed because they were the evidence of the androgyne Deity and had been respected as such in ancient cultures. And the mentally ill had to be killed because of the ancient tradition that considered insanity to be indicative of being touched by God, so that even today, the enraptured devotee of Shiva may act in the manner of one who is insane, since closeness to divinity results in the realization that nothing in this life really matters.

The Aryan religious system, devoid of the Green aspect, was dedicated to a God of fire who dwelled on a mountain; it was a patriarchal system with the males being in touch with the supreme deity through fire worship and sacrifices; and it was patrilineal with inheritance by the males and, subsequently, male dominance over the females (no matter how benevolent or equitable), maintained through the requirement of monogamy solely for females and their exclusion from performing the rite of the sacrifice.

Hitler had an ambitious plan to literally reverse the flow of history by taking his race back to what he considered to be its pure form. He recognized that people had been conditioned by centuries of religious instruction and religious wars to faithfully believe in what he knew was an "impure" religion. His reputation for being intrigued with archaeology and the occult points to his determination to find proof that the pure form of Aryanism was superior, but all his experts actually discovered was that Aryanism was the religion of a people becoming organized to fight for expansion. This led Hitler, toward the end of his power, to declare that he would take the world out in a conflagration with no regard to any race, not even his own.

His efforts at purification did not meet with great resistance because he was careful about the order in which his purges took place. Not very many people complained about the destruction of the mentally ill—they were expensive to maintain in asylums during the Depression. Not many others complained about the labeling of homosexuals—they were denounced by all mainstream religions already. Not many complained about the treatment of the Gypsies—they were alien and suspect in their mysterious living habits, and besides, most were probably thieves anyway. When the Jews were labeled and then rounded up, it was just another unwanted group. People had been reduced to "types," and this lack of identity as individuals made it easier for the Nazis to isolate and launch attacks against large segments of the population in stages that were acceptable to the general population.

The fact that modern religionists have since pointed to the Bible as predicting the rise of a Hitler is not realistic—the Bible was written for its own self-preservation, and the rebellion against its tenets was expected because there was always the chance that someone would try to revert to the original Sind-based religions at the very time of the writings. This was a case of contemporary injunctions against the current religious situation and denouncements in advance, warning the devotees of the impure Aryan system to fight for their religion. It was not expected, however (and this in itself disproves the "prophetic" nature of Scripture), that the rebellion would come from Aryan purists.

The problem with what are generally accepted in modern times as mainstream religions is that they are basically a corruption of the older systems. All are based in pantheism, as Arnold Toynbee saw it, and any attempt to return to a purer form of the nature religions is seen by mainstream religions both as threatening and heretical. The truth is, however, that the mainstream religions are the heretical aspects of older religious forms, and exist by threatening revivals of their antecedents, be it by burning Witches at the stake or by utilizing the vast tax-free resources of modern religions for widespread use of the media to revile Neo-Paganism and instill a fear in people of non-mainstream religions and their practices. Blatant, hysteria-inducing name-calling and false claims about doctrinal differences are evidence of the fearfulness produced by the old beliefs in those who have a vested interest in maintaining ignorance of the origins of mainstream religions. The scapegoating of Pagans and Witches by Fundamentalist groups serves solely as a means of uniting people in a manufactured cause against changing awareness and education. By providing something relatively harmless, like the general term of Paganism, as a focus for rage and hatred, all the ills of society can be seen as stemming from religious nonconformists rather than from mainstream religious views, the individuals themselves, or their outmoded social structure.

Wiccans and other Neo-Pagans are labeled by many mainstream religionists as Satanists, Nazis, evil, and perverse, when in truth, all these Pagans are doing is accepting the oneness humankind shares with the Earth and the Universe; accepting the duality of divinity and equality of all humans, male and female, of all colors. They can see how, as genetic people living on and integrated with the Earth (which is itself seen to be a living organism), humans can be expected to evolve and experience changes in spiritual, physical, and mental development.

Variations in human expression are not seen as threatening by Pagans. Unlike many mainstream religions, the need for conformity is not a prerequisite for acceptance. Life forms are as different as the interplay of basic genetic harmonics permits, and this gives rise to the various expressions of human sexuality, creativity, intelligence, and physical characteristics. There are infinite possibilities to human adaptation and change, which does not alarm Neo-Pagans or Wiccans because of their sense of being in balance with all nature, but typically does alarm the mainstream religionists because their sense of being depends on the power they can claim, based on the amount of community conformity to their faith. Thus, while one never hears a Pagan telling someone that he/she will go to hell (because the Pagan knows that the only hell that exists is the one a person creates for him/herself), that threat is used to keep participants in the mainstream cohesive.

The connection between the occult (hidden knowledge), Paganism, and Nazism is not what has traditionally been presented. The matter is much more complex. The Gypsy tradition, that of Witchcraft and mages, and the religions that developed from the Indus, were the enemy to Hitler. What modern religionists do not want to face is that Hitler placed them in the same category as Witches and Pagan Gypsies—the very people that Christians and Jews have themselves been known to discriminate against and persecute—and they do not want to accept that they are themselves the products of these repudiated belief systems. Hitler may well have seen that connection and wanted to correct what he perceived as the mistake made by the Aryans. The Aryan minority conquered civilized people by means of their superior weapons and techniques of war, but once in a position of power, they were literally surrounded by their foes. In order to rule, they had to integrate those they had conquered into a workable power structure—and religion was the perfect tool. Their only failure was that the integration worked both ways, and elements of the local religions became infused into the Aryan system.

Judaism represents the first remarkable attempt to purge the Aryan system of pre-Aryan, Vanir-level beliefs, but this was not truly successful until after the Christian adaptation of Judaism occurred and lent support to the relevancy of the Jewish faith by active Christian destruction of Pagan sources. It was the unequivocal acceptance of the Old Testament as literal truth by the Christians that reinforced the maintenance of Judaism, even to the extent of forcibly giving the land of Palestine to the Jews for a homeland called Israel, and continuing the support of that nation through financial and technical aid in current times (over three billion dollars yearly from the United States government, and this does not include private fund-raising in America).

The Fundamentalist Christian support of Israel reflects a desperation to have Bible prophecy fulfilled. The end result of fulfillment is interpreted as bringing the faithful into the position of world domination after the annihilation of billions of hapless nonbelievers in a variety of horrors from which the faithful will be blissfully absent (the "Rapture" concept of Christianity). It is this notion of nonparticipation in the results of their violent activities that makes the Fundamentalist movements of any sect dangerous—they feel that they have nothing to lose and will not have to face the consequences of their actions. When it becomes apparent that all the Jews will not return to Israel, whether it be because they are at home in their adopted land or simply do not want to live in the Near East, the next event will be a persecution of recalcitrant Jews in order to force history into the misunderstood mold of the New Testament Revelation. It is this kind of ignorance of ancient cosmologies that has twisted the making of history for nearly 2,000 years. Thus it was that, from Hitler's point of view, the Christian religions were as much a pollution to the Aryan faith as the Jewish religion.

The earliest failure of Aryan religious purity came from India, and from this land came the Gypsies who left their indelible imprint on the Slavs. When the Aryans invaded India and displaced Shiva, they must have been surprised to see how this deity retained His power over the hearts and minds of the local people. Even when He was insulted and degraded in early Aryan (Vedic) mythology, He endured. His calm, unperturbed demeanor captivated His conquerors until he displaced their own mountain deity, Indra, as one part of the Vedic Trinity. His status was then upgraded in a succession of myths that now stand in perplexing contrast to one another. Yet even this is seen as a positive aspect of the power of Shiva—one cannot destroy the Destroyer—and in time one must recognize that He is also the Creator who dances the Eternal Dance of life and death and life again. If the Aryans had been successful in eradicating all belief in Shiva at the outset, they might have altered the history of India and that of the world. There might have been no impetus for the creation of Judaism, Christianity, or Islam. These historically recent religions only came about because the influence of Shiva and Shakti continued to threaten the power of the Aryan priesthood by infiltrating the Aryan religion.

The revival of Teutonic Paganism in German society by Hitler was gradual, but deliberate. His concept of genetic purity of the race is consistent with Teutonic Paganism, but taken to the extreme. Ancestry and genetics figure in the Teutonic belief of the soul passing down a family line, so that the belief in reincarnation is not just that of rebirth, but rebirth into the specific family, tribe, and race. Thorsson feels that the Jungian idea of archetypes shows this same transmission through genetic inheritance rather than simply through cultural heritage. With Neo-Paganism today, there is an element of this in the Odinist (or Asatru) Pagans. They do not consider themselves part of the general Neo-Pagan movement, do not incorporate the ideas of Witchcraft or Eastern beliefs, and do not seek racial integration in their system. For many of them, following the Odinist system means that reincarnation will occur in the genetic family unit, and this makes it necessary to prevent dilution of the blood with outsiders, while also making propagation and sons (to carry on the family name) an obligation.

The religion itself is insulated from non-Odinist deities and concepts. Hence, it does not incorporate astrology, Tarot, kabbalah, or chakras into the practices. Instead, Odinists turn to the Scandinavian, Norse, and Germanic deities (of which Odin is a predominant figure). These Pagans today sometimes find themselves compared to Nazis or attracting people who have Nazi leanings because of their emphasis on ancestral roots. Yet Teutonic Paganism can not be blamed as the culprit or cause of Nazism, any more than Christianity can be blamed or seen as the cause of the Inquisition. What people in power *do* with religion is what causes atrocities.

Modern Odinists tend to believe in "live and let live" while yet maintaining exclusivity; they wonder why anyone not of Scandinavian, Norse, and Germanic heritage would even consider the Asatru path and feel such people should seek their own roots. But racial awareness can become very sticky when one considers the possibilities for intermarriages and unions over the past few millennia and even in recent centuries in America. That was why Hitler created his farms for racially pure "human stock"—his ideal blond-haired, blue-eyed children created from genetic matings of pairs deemed suitable by his geneticists—to start over with what would become a "purebred" race of people. It is dangerous for Neo-Pagans to proudly point out their heritage today and make this a factor for isolation in their own religious path when they cannot be certain that one of their own offspring might not betray a genetic mixture from their buried past or create a new characteristic through natural genetic mutation that does not fall within accepted parameters. It is likely that this aspect of Aryan Paganism did not exist in the original practice of religion until their warlike migrations brought the Aryan invaders into contact with a diversity of peoples and beliefs; and so the true bloodlines are as subject to infiltration as anywhere else.

It is the element of exclusivity that distinguishes the Teutonic Paganism of Hitler and the religion of the Aryan invaders of India and the Near East from the regional beliefs of the people they conquered. It was this concept of exclusiveness that created the Brahmins of Hinduism and the Levites of Judaism, and encouraged the schism in Islam over whether the religion must be run by descendants and relatives of Mohammed or by anyone of Islamic belief. The Shiites are the ones who accept rulership only from the family of Mohammed (in true Aryan tradition), while the Sunnites accept the rulership of any man who has studied the faith and advanced in religious degrees to a point where he has gained the respect of his fellow devotees (in the Sind tradition except for the subjugation of women, which is not Sind, but Aryan). From these two views of Aryanism, the world now sees the results in the wars between Shiite Iran (ancient Persia) and Sunnite Iraq (ancient Sumeria and Babylonia).

The Jews can be seen as following the Aryan tradition of exclusivity by their acceptance of the hereditary rulership of the Levites, while Christians may be seen as "living in Sind" for allowing themselves to be ruled in religious matters by anyone who holds the position of church elder, pastor, reverend, and so forth.

The closest that Christianity comes to emulating the exclusivity of the Aryans is in the denominational rivalries that cause different sects to claim salvation as belonging only to their particular members. The Roman Catholic Church grants the title of Pope in the same authority as a hereditary Aryan ruler, for the Pope is the infallible ruler of that branch of Christianity, but Popes themselves are elected and not genetically related. Mormons have reinstated the Aryan element of exclusivity into their corporate form of Christianity through a system of rulership by the twelve patriarchs—descendants of the original followers of Joseph Smith. They also advocate the use of family genealogical studies of the membership for the purpose of baptizing relatives into the faith, alive or dead, willing or unwilling—all for a price.

It was because of the predominance of Italian leadership in the Catholic Church, and its incorporation of many Goddess elements into its liturgy, that Hitler planned to strike them next, and he doubtless felt that he would have the support of anti-Catholic Protestants in this persecution. Next would come the turn of the

Christian Protestants to be eradicated. Only then could Aryan Paganism be fully restored, with the new race especially created for him. The Christianized version of Aryan exclusivity (warring over doctrinal differences, with each sect claiming to be the only sect that is faithful to Scripture and "saved") was what allowed the German people and others of Europe to passively accept the Holocaust. The fact that the people most visible in the persecutions were themselves exclusive because of Aryan influence is an ironic contrast to the plight of the non-Aryan Gypsies.

The real battle between Aryan and non-Aryan Pagan belief systems should have been a moot point in a modern world, yet the battles of 2000 B.C.E. were resurrected in the early years of the twentieth century C.E. What Hitler was attempting to do was go back in time and correct the mistakes of earlier Aryan conquerors, to eliminate the infusion of non-Aryan beliefs into the Teutonic system. The results, had he succeeded, would have been staggering. Imagine then, the religious systems, one linked with a political system, degenerating into two basic fronts—the purely Aryan, political religion of the mountain, patriarchal Father God, against the non-Aryan, nature religion of earth-fertility, matriarchal Mother Goddess and Her Consort, the gentle, loving Horned God. Yet this is exactly the scenario that is anticipated in Biblical prophecies. This is not prophecy, but the recognition of Levite priests by 621 B.C.E. of the potential power of the oppressed victims of Aryan conquest. One must remember that the Bible is an Aryan tool.

From the Judeo-Christian perspective, Hitler then becomes the hero of the Aryan (and therefore, Levite) cause, by supporting the Father God and Aryan patriarchal system of the Old Testament. He becomes the champion of Christian revelation in his fight against the worship of the Mother Goddess in the Catholic Church (called Mary, the Mother of God), and in restoring to purity the Aryan faith, sullied by Hebrew Semites who dared to name themselves "the Chosen People" while excluding Germanic Aryans from this honorific title. It is all a matter of interpretation, and Hitler was able to use this fact to accomplish the horrors of genocidal extermination.

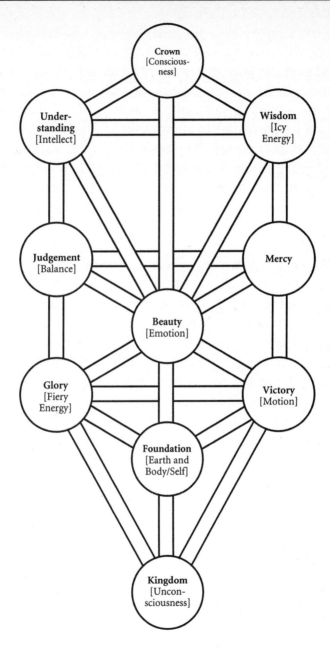

The Kabbalah and the Nine Realms of Yggdrasill arranged to show the matchings between the two: Beauty and Mercy are combined as emotion in the Teutonic system, hence nine rather than ten realms.

There were many people who closed their minds to the murder of innocents because they were caught up in a holy cause; a predestined and God-ordained holy wrath. The absurdity continues to this day. It was Christian Fundamentalist ministers in America who cheered the war in Kuwait and Iraq as evidence of the end of the world—they were willing to allow millions of people to die so that their own "Rapture" could be pushed into being. But there was no Armageddon, just loss of life and despoiling of the waterways. The cheer died out, but the sad part is that cruelty, violence, death, and earthly destruction are eagerly desired for others by some Christian Fundamentalists, in the hope that this will lead to their being carried up into heaven. It was this kind of perverse pessimism ingrained in Christianity that Hitler used to gain his objectives.

It was only after they stopped and surveyed the damage that people realized the enormity of their error. The Germans were not alone in this, for there were many people worldwide who supported or condoned these exterminations and felt empathy for this intolerance because they saw it as predicted in the Bible. People were used because they were conditioned by religion to anticipate righteous mayhem through a garbled interpretation of the Bible, and when they were confronted with the reality of what they had done, they turned away in shame. Today, one would be hard pressed to find anyone in Germany, for example, who will admit to ever supporting Hitler—yet the throngs of his followers can be seen to number in the hundreds of thousands in old film footage. Hitler could present himself as a Biblical hero to his supporters throughout the Western world. When mythology is taken as history and as a genuine prophecy from a divine source, reason is shut down, and intolerance is given sway. During World War II the Bible was used to popularize anti-Semitism; today it is used to promote homophobia and anti-feminism.

One can see a more peaceful recognition of the two ancient religious traditions in modern Neo-Paganism. Why should one branch be prone to exclusiveness while the other is open to the integration of human kind? The clue lies in the geographic location of their development. Here then is the heritage of the Sun People and the Ice People as recently expounded upon in university settings. Whichever path one follows depends upon individual preference and heritage. People with a Nordic, Scandinavian, and Germanic heritage might be inclined to the Celtic Tradition, but it is more likely that being familiar with the gods and goddesses of the Vikings, they would gravitate to the Asatru. People from areas of Europe that were influenced by the Celts and Indus travelers would tend to gravitate toward the deities of their ancestors—Mother Goddess, the Horned God, and others. People from the more southern regions of Africa would gravitate toward their own ancestral deities, some of which have distinctly Indus touches acquired through contacts in prehistory times and from the integrated southern societies of those days. People of the Far East have a different heritage that contains aspects of the Indus tradition in the Yin and Yang, as well as localized beliefs that are Aryan regarding ancestor worship. But such a tendency is problematical due to the nonorganizational aspect of Neo-Paganism. Thus there is always the possibility for the formation of a group of Black Odinists!

As long as the ugly specter of "superiority" does not get a foothold in Neo-Paganism, all the Pagan systems, be they Aryan, shamanic, kabbalistic, or Wiccan, should thrive together. The primary key to the modern success of the Pagan revival is the unifying belief that each person is free to follow his/her own path, and that all paths are equally valid. The need for a concept of "superiority" came from the political aspirations of a man intent on regressing (before changing) history. Racial and ethnic superiority were the enabling tools of a dictatorship that hoped to eventually destroy the very people being deluded with praise of their greatness, in order to replace them with Hitler's genetically screened children.

The reason Hitler was doomed to failure from the start was because, in the end, he could not create quickly enough, nor maintain, a segregated system and win in a war against a homogenized nation like the United States of America. The ancient Northern and Southern cultures were too integrated in America for the Aryan cause to be palatable. There were too many people of Italian, German, Irish,

Hispanic, French, and Native American descent in its armed forces for America to be divided into Aryan and non-Aryan regions.

Orientals and Negroes were not factored into the equation, for the battle lines were based primarily on a conflict of European worship systems. Also, in Hitler's time, the Armed Forces of the United States were still not fully integrated, and African-Americans were the subject of segregation in many facets of daily life in America. This also explains why Neo-Nazis see a need for a separate region set aside for white supremacists. They want to retain the Aryan past and the Aryan Pagan system of genetic reincarnation and patriarchal inheritance, but in the face of modern trends toward the empowerment of African-Americans and women, interracial unions, the acceptability of women retaining their surnames and having matrilineal descent through non-marriage (single mothers), and the need for multicultural studies in schools because of the shrinking of the world through mass communications, the Aryan supremacist is foundering in what he or she sees as an eroding social structure that once supported the Aryan ideals of male dominance and racial segregation. These same factors are what Fundamentalist Christians and Orthodox Jews have focused on to name religious nonconformists as scapegoats for the modern social changes that threaten to erode their power base.

The Neo-Pagan and Wiccan trend toward eclecticism can be traced to the intermarriages of various ethnic peoples. Most Americans are a combination of cultural backgrounds rather than purely Irish, or German, or Italian, etc., and thus can easily assimilate a variety of deity concepts into one workable path. The tendency toward eclectic traditions in Europe stems from the same intercultural unions, as well as awareness brought about through the mass media and migrations of peoples from former (or current) colonial possessions.

It may well be that the reason the Neo-Pagan/Wiccan movement has become so popular in recent years is that the authority of mainstream religions has been undermined by a combination of more education; discoveries in the fields of history and archaeology;

and the ability to spread the associated ideas through printed matter, television, and movies. Mainstream religions cannot maintain
their suffocating grip on the minds of the populace once college-
level education is available to the masses, and the ideas inherent in
Paganism and the New Age are no longer kept out of bookstores, the
press, and television. (Recent examples are the airing of the Shirley
McLaine film, *Out On A Limb,* and various talk shows wherein
guests speak positively about Neo-Paganism and Wicca, as well as
Public Broadcasting Station shows like *Testament* and the *Myth*
series of Joseph Campbell.)

Writers like J. R. R. Tolkien strike a nerve by presenting an
alternative reality that works in its own framework and meshes with
the tenuous fibers of human history, thus demonstrating how one
person can create a myth that will appeal to millions. Joseph Campbell's intriguing series of books and lectures on human mythological systems forced people to realize that the themes of modern
Judeo-Christian religions were not exclusive and not the word of
any one god, but a collective and unifying mythological experience
of all peoples, worshipping many deities in different ways. The
monopoly on Western thought held by the Christian churches is
being broken, and as time goes on the only possible path is one of
further divergence from mainstream religions.

In order to avert this loss of power and control, the churches
will have either to bend to include the ideals of the Neo-Pagans in
their own liturgy, or attempt to terrify their followers and insulate
them from knowledge and public education—both paths are currently in evidence in varying degrees in a number of churches. The
only other option, which is not truly viable, is warfare against nonconformists. The advent of mass migrations and the flux of population, with a variety of ethnic backgrounds represented in many
countries, make this an unwieldy course, one that could result in
civil wars of religion all over the world, with the ultimate power
going to whichever country had the most ethnically insulated
group—perhaps Japan or China—and without the need for effort
to be expended in conquest. Even a victory for orthodoxy would be

a defeat because of the high cost of such a war with today's weapons. Everyone would be affected, and everyone would know that the cause was based on intolerance, in direct violation of Western democratic and constitutional tradition.

Today there are religious wars in various locations around the world—Irish Catholics against Protestants, Indian Moslems against Hindus, Hindus against Buddhists, Shiite Moslems against anyone not Shiite, Moslems against Jews, and Christians against Moslems in Eastern Europe. Already, world opinion decries these senseless massacres of innocent people who are the pawns of political leaders divorced from the suffering they inflict upon others, or driven by fanaticism to not care. With education and the spread of knowledge concerning the roots of these conflicts, people may come to realize that religion is only a cover for the real cause for wars—that wars are political and economic, involving power and control, not spiritual salvation. When taken in that context, the people can see that wars come from greed, that invoking the name of a deity is no excuse for killing, because there is nothing sacred about human avarice. Perhaps then people would be less likely to be swayed by artificial bigotry, and the result would be a shaking of faith in any religion that deliberately demanded such destructiveness. This, in turn, would generate appreciation for a more tolerant, Earth-centered path of duality. The better aspects of the old Paganism could receive a worldwide revival.

The advent of mass education could help to forestall further civil wars of religion and give nations an opportunity to recognize that conflicts rooted in ethnic differences come from not understanding the oneness of humanity. These conflicts, then, are most likely to occur in regions where intercultural education has either been neglected or perverted to support a regime that would otherwise fail or be forced into accepting changes. In the case of modern Japan, there is much publicity about the America bashing going on in that country, but the cause is not readily addressed. That cause stems from the foreign contacts and tourism currently occurring. For the most part, the Japanese government (and the corporations that finance it) has tried to keep Japanese tourists isolated from American citizens and has directly supported Japanese-owned and operated resorts in foreign lands to cater to their people.

Nevertheless, students coming to America (and those going from America to Japan), commercial and cultural exchanges, and tourists who opt to see the country without being tied to a Japanese agenda, are making contacts that allow the Japanese people to discover another people who have a different perspective on World War II, who have better homes and luxuries, have education for all instead of just a selected few, and have the benefits of unions and legal rights to prevent corporations from reducing them to modern serfdom.

The message is filtering into Japan that things could be done differently, that Japanese education is not as great as some people like to think—the tradition of ending high school history courses with the late nineteenth century is hardly useful for a nation about to enter the twenty-first century—and that there is something for Japanese workers to learn from Americans. This is what motivates the "old guard" to revile Americans and make ethnic slurs against the varieties of cultures represented in America. The notion being presented is not for overseas, but for the people in Japan—isolation is presented as good, and racial superiority is supported to preserve the power of the current rulers.

In Eastern European countries, ethnic fighting in recently de-Communized countries is the result of the population not being kept abreast of the movement of ideas and cultural exchanges. They have lived in a vacuum, under repressive governments for nearly fifty years, and have burst forth from their bounds with the mentality of the early nineteenth century. In the Near East, nations that had known freedom of ideas and advancement have become strangled with the ideologies of an exclusive religion used by people seeking power and control to subvert the education that would otherwise nullify their powerbase.

So what can be the future of religion in the world? Can a personal mythology be the answer? It can be only with the general recognition that no one path is superior to another. It is likely that most Neo-Pagans and Wiccans already accept this tenet, and that there will never be an "orthodox" path established. Each individual must seek to find the Divine within—individually—soul to Soul. With the Neo-Pagan movement gaining momentum, opposition will increase, but the powerbase of the "Church" is eroded in America, *by design,* in the mandated separation of state and church. This is what gives America the edge in exploring new spiritual ground. The Founding Fathers (and Mothers) knew what they were doing; knew that it was wrong to legislate another's soul or conscience. It would seem that ultimately the Neo-Pagan movement must be successful because it will work inside people and cause them to be more loving and accepting of one another. People cannot preach against that without exposing a base of self-hatred and irrational fear of others. That is what makes Neo-Paganism the better alternative.

Bringing It All Together

From the evidence gathered through archaeology it has become apparent that Shiva is the oldest continuously worshiped deity known to human society. He was the basis for widespread natural religious beliefs, which incorporated veneration of the phallus, vagina/womb, horns, bulls, snakes, and trees, dating from the Paleolithic period until around 4,000 years ago when a political religious system developed.

In contemporary Hinduism, just as in pre-Vedic times, Shiva has been depicted as both male and female combined (Ardhanari) or separated into two aspects as Shiva (male) and Shakti (female). The name for God traditionally is AUM or UMA, depending upon which aspect is being addressed and, in a way later echoed by the Hebraic kabbalah tradition, has meaning in each letter. Tantric Hinduism has it that the A equates to "Grace" (male), U is "Power" (female), and M is the "All" (androgyne). The term AUM (also written in modern Hinduism as "OM" and used as a powerful mantra with a pronunciation that incorporates all the vowel sounds) is identified as male Shiva, with the emphasis on the aescetic "Grace." But the female aspect of UMA, seen in modern India, as well as ancient Sind and early Sumer and Babylon, is the name of the Goddess with the aspect of "Power" being emphasized. Nevertheless, Shiva is Shakti, and Shakti is Shiva, and They are both united in either name by the "All," which is Shiva and Shakti as androgyne.

The ancient term "Dravidic" is generally applied to the Indus people who lived in the Sind region before the advent of the Aryan invaders. Today there are a distinct regional people in Southern India known as Dravidic, and they are considered to be descended from the refugees who fled the Indus during the invasions. These people today still worship the Goddess as primary, with Shiva as Her consort being secondary to Her "Power." Both the Dravidic Shiva of the Indus and the Shiva of modern Hinduism are still often portrayed as hermaphrodites, and this image was carried by migrating Dravidians to various parts of the Western world by at least 6000 B.C.E., as evidenced by Neolithic Eastern and Mediterranean European artifacts and burial customs.

In both ancient artworks of India and modern statues, Shiva is sometimes depicted as split down the middle, head to toe, with the right side being male and the left side being female (see photo on page 23). That is why modern Wiccan altars generally will place the God on the viewer's right and the Goddess on the viewer's left—to make the positioning accurate from the viewer's perspective. This veneration of a Dual Deity is one of the basic differences between the practices of Witches and those of the Teutonic Pagans.

Witchcraft hearkens back to the worship familiar to the people of the Indus some 30,000 years ago, while the Teutonic practice, without reference to the equally female aspect of the Deity, dates to a little over 4,000 years ago and represents a different evolution of worship. For the Teutonic, the difference in lifestyle brought about by a need for expansion, and the subsequent development of a warring and ruling hierarchy, resulted in a specialized clergy whose duty it was to validate this system by standing between the ruled and their deities. The limitations of the Northern environment may also have resulted in an emphasis on the value of brute strength needed for the protection of females and young in the harsh life at the edge of the Ice Age. Yet, as Danilou and Toynbee postulate, the new system brought about a man-centeredness and signaled the end of living with respect toward nature and the environment.

Religion everywhere had been based in nature and ecstasy, but the new version was based in ritual and a newly defined morality which served as a means of controlling people. No longer were people part of the Divine process of nature, but separate, and given the injunction to dominate without thought for the future, since there was only final judgment and eternal bliss or eternal damnation. Because of this attitude, enforced by civil law, dogmas stifled individual self-realization and destroyed the intrinsic joy of being part of the Divine through living the creation. The attacks on sexuality were defined through lack of any other suitable teaching; it provided a "scapegoat" focus for people who were, by law and clergy, no longer allowed to participate in the sacred firsthand. The individually felt and expressed magic of the past was reduced, through the power of the clergy, into mere public ritual.

In post-Dravidic Hindu tradition, OM is the Supreme Being in the form of sound and comes at the start and end (alpha and omega) of all hymns, religious actions, and recitations of sacred text (similar to "Amen"). It is the most powerful of all mantras and is spelled AUM in the Tantric tradition of Hinduism, which is believed to be based on the tradition of Sind. This relates to the mainstream Christian view of the power of the Word of God; Judaic inhibition against speaking or writing the Name of God; and the use of "words of power" by ancient Pagans and the Neo-Pagans of today. Mantras were adopted into use by kabbalah, and subsequent ceremonialist, magic traditions, in the sense that people tried to use these ancient sounds (mantras or words of power) to make the gods subject to the will of the practitioners.

In the Vedic tradition, with its attempt to suppress the Dravidic, the meanings of the letters of AUM were changed into "Wakefulness," "Dreaming," and "Deep Sleep," with the whole being "Transcendance." The fact that the more ancient tradition was not lost speaks to the resiliency of the Old Religion. The powerful concept of male and female in union as equals, as Shiva/Shakti, was too appealing an image to be swept aside by the Aryan deities of Brahma, Vishnu, and Indra. Instead, Indra was diminished, and the male Shiva was given a place in the Triad, with Shakti relegated to the position of His spouse in the male-oriented religion.

The Aryans worked hard to discourage the worship of the Horned God, the Lord of the Beasts, the God of Fertility, the Lord of the Dance, by aligning Shiva with their own negative deity, Rudra, and giving Him new aspects in their mythology—Lord of Vampires, Terror, and Destroyer. Nevertheless, over the centuries, the mythologies changed to reflect Shiva's endurance and advancement in the religion of the people who conquered the Dravidians. Today, Shiva devotees see Him as the embodiment of Love (the modern metaphor of "God is Love" came from the Hindu statement, "Shiva is Love" some 200 years earlier), and affirm that Brahma and Vishnu are merely aspects of Shiva, who is All. Some Tantric versions emphasize "Power" over "Grace," call Shakti the primary deity, and revere Her as Devi, the Mother Goddess, Great Goddess, and many other forms still seen today in modern India. The origins of religious tradition in Mesopotamia can be traced to the Indus River Valley with the worship of Shiva and Devi (male and female, grace and power) in one aspect or another. It was to refute the God and the Goddess that the Judaic system was devised; thus does Judaism owe its beginnings to Shiva/Shakti. The very word "God" comes from the German *Gott,* which Danielou sees as derived from the Sanskrit root, *Go,* meaning "the bull"; while the French and Latin version of *Dieu* is derived from the word *Div,* meaning "radiant"— the same as Deva ("Shining One"), and in description, the same as the term applied to the Fairie Folk, Sidhe (*Siddha,* "charged with energy"). In these ways it becomes clear that the popular deity image of the Old Religion is still retained in the vocabulary of modern mainstream religions.

Western religion today reflects an amalgam created by the intersection of Aryan practices and beliefs with those of ancient Sind. The Aryan aspects can be traced by reverting and retrogressing to the themes constant in Christ, Buddha, Krishna, Indra, Thor, and Odin.

The Baptism of Jesus

The themes of Sind are found by taking what is left. If negative, the theme reflects an Aryan rebuke of a Sind practice or belief. If incorporated into the overall system, the theme reflects a Sind aspect, absorbed and tolerated, if not always accepted by the Aryans, to form the conglomerate of modern religions. Thus, there are three components in modern Western religious beliefs: (1. Aryanism; (2. Sind; and (3. Aryan rejection of Sind. Since parts of Sind were accepted, these aspects were aligned with the religion of the Aryans and have effectively become identified as Aryan. From that point, whatever was rejected was labeled Sind, to become modern sin.

Included in the accepted Sind practices are ritual bathing, water baptism, an all-powerful yet personal God, a dutiful and nurturing consort/Mother, a Holy Spirit, accessibility of the God and the Mother of God by the masses through personal prayer and gifts (be it lighting candles, presenting flowers, or burning incense), and the concepts or practices centered around the idea of God being within the individual, rebirth through the union with the Holy Spirit, and unity with God. These are features that are absent from pure Aryanism.

Aspects of pure Aryanism include the use of an altar and fire sacrifices (be it animal or human) to appease God; a God of wrath and vengeance approachable only by a selected priesthood; ritual words, motions, and adornments; temple artifacts, priesthood duties, ritual attonements, and rewards codified into a holy law; holy laws as the sum of mundane existence, with penalties for disobedience placed in the hands of the administering priesthood; a Savior to redeem a people considered naturally evil; a Heaven where the "saved" labor for God and praise God continuously; and a Hell where the "unsaved" are eternally tortured.

Aspects of Sind rejected by Aryanism and labeled as "sin" (derived from "Sind" as previously explained) involve the power of the Goddess (who was generally made male and designated as a demon or devil); snakes as symbols of immortality and wisdom, being made evil in the Bible version of Creation; ready availability of eternal life symbolized by a tree, of whose fruit Adam and Eve were forbidden to partake; manifestations of the energies inhabiting plants, animals, and minerals, with devas becoming demons and evil spirits; independent women, who are personified as a variety of contemptible, threatening, or homicidal demonesses like Jezebel, the succubus, and Lilith; freedom of the individual to approach God on a level of daily life without a special holy day each week or pre-scribed rituals involving an ordained clergy, such people being labeled as heretics and eliminated through war, torture, and execu-tion; the inherent goodness of people and sexuality being consid-ered normal, these being specifically repudiated in doctrine that is enforced through religious and/or civil law; and the right to enjoy life without fear of a hell (or even a heaven), for the law of Karma lays the responsibility and repayment for one's actions on oneself, rejected by dogma in the Judeo-Christian-Islamic system, but accepted in the Buddhist system. Hinduism, as a closer combination of Aryanism and Sind, is more erratic in the acceptance of Sind tra-ditions, and any of these aspects entering into the Aryanized faith becomes a component for one of the various denominations of Hinduism.

Thus, "sin" comes from following the religion of Sind, which is merely the name of that region of the Indus Valley which lies direct-ly across from the mouth of the Gulf of Oman, at the top of the Ara-bian Sea, from whence came the religion of Shiva and Shakti. Even the Goddess Ishtar's father was named Sin in Babylonian mytholo-gy. Archaeological evidence shows that there was abundant trade between the advanced region of India and the less well-developed regions of Arabia, Iran, and Iraq around 2900 B.C.E., and as it is con-sidered likely that the earlier Sumerians of 3600 B.C.E. were colonists from Sind. It would therefore have been natural for Sind to be a major influence on the religious development in the area.

The devil, then, is merely an antagonistic view of the Goddess, or Devi, of Dravidian belief. The name of David applied to the "House of God" can be traced to the far more ancient name of the Dravidic people and their religion. As their beliefs formed the basis for the most ancient religion known in Mesopotamia, the Dravidians were themselves the "House of God"—the people from whom the concepts of the dual Deity originated. By 2000 B.C.E., the Dravidians worshiped Shiva in the aspect of a Tree God, and Devi was a Tree Goddess, which reflects the influence of the heavy forestation of the Indus region and the importance of woodcarving skills among the inhabitants. Devi was also identified with snakes—the venom being most likely used for oracles and divination purposes. Saul, Israel's alleged first king, is a name for a durable and prized tree of India, and David succeeds this "Tree" (of the Goddess) as Dravidic Shiva (male aspect assuming Aryan "Power").

The writers of the Bible frequently turned female deities into males (Goddess Ashtoreth becoming the male demon Astaroth, for example) and distortions in names were deliberately used to prevent the Aryan Yahweh from being compared to a female. Thus Saul actually represents the female tree of the Goddess Devi, while She then became a male devil. This is all a metaphor expressing the transition of the Semite Hebrews through stages into a Judaic religion. David weds Bathsheba ("daughter of Shiva") to fully subordinate the female aspect of Shiva. Their son Solomon is, in mythical terms, the first Aryan king of the Hebrews, and is called peaceful and wise. Why was David's dancing into Jerusalem before the Ark of the Covenant deemed wrong in the Bible story? Because it showed that Dravidic Shiva, Lord of the Dance, entered the region before an Aryan deity could be established.

Why did the Queen of Sheba (Shiva's Queen) come to Solomon? So the Aryan king could demonstrate the superiority of Judaism by sending Shiva's wife ("Power") to wed an obscure mortal king and be submissive to him. Shiva's aspect of wisdom is fully integrated into Solomon and the Aryan religion here, and Shakti is depicted as mortal and vanquished in the light of Aryan supremacy. These were not historic events, and archaeologists and historians today recognize this, present this in professional journals and books, and show this on cable and public television programs, but make little or no headway in the instruction of today's youth, because history textbooks are regulated by mainstream religion activists.

The Old Testament is only a myth used to bolster the importance of a new religion in the minds of the early Semite people called Hebrews. These people, in reality, were very eclectic in their religious practices. Any reading of the Bible shows that the Levite priesthood was constantly struggling to keep their subjects from reverting to the religious customs that predated Judaism. One must also keep in mind that the Old Testament was not even begun until 621 B.C.E.; that the New Testament was not formulated until circa 400 C.E., and that Christian orthodoxy was still being debated after the Second Council of Constantinople in 553 C.E. Meanwhile, the Pagan traditions of the Old Religion were being practiced, the Pagan holidays were being observed, and the Pagan deities were being honored by the vast majority of the population.

Solomon receiving the Queen of Sheba

Why does Christian tradition say that God is "three in one"? Because Shiva is traditionally called Trimurti ("Three-Embodied"). Why does Satan have a pitchfork? Because Shiva's symbol (painted on the foreheads of devotees at ceremonies) is the trident, which shows the Trimurti aspect by having three points joined into one weapon. This is also the Gae Bulga, the "Fairie weapon" given to the Irish hero of Ulster, Cuchulainn, whose father was supposed to be of the Fairie people. It was a weapon a Dravidic father would give to his half-Celtic son; the trident symbol of his Dravidic God.

Why was the widespread Hebrew veneration of cows and worship of the golden calf (as related in Exodus) a practice denounced by Levite priests? Because the cow is sacred to Shakti in Her aspect of Danu, and the bull is sacred to Shiva as his mount, Nandi, who is still accorded great reverence in India today. Why did sexual relations become a "sin" (something from Sind)? Because Shiva's Linga and Shakti's Yoni are the representations of fertility and the pleasure of creation. And why does Satan have horns—indeed why a Horned God throughout Western European Pagan and Wiccan history? Because this is the depiction of Shiva as Lord of the Beasts (Shiva Pasupati), known for 30,000 years, and carried into the Near East and the European continent as the image of the God of animals and nature.

People who call themselves Bible historians (which is often a contradiction in terms) claim that the Israelites settled in Egypt to escape a famine, circa 1500 B.C.E.; yet at that time the Aryans were initiating their destruction of the lower Indus Valley civilization and assaulting Mohenjo-daro until its fall in 1250 B.C.E. Could the later arriving Levite (Aryan) priesthood have experienced some of their difficulties controlling their Hebrew flock due to the migrations of Dravidians who had earlier fled the destruction of their cities? Their presence would aggravate the tenuous grip the Levites had on the Hebrews, and result in a number of resurgent Dravidic practices among the people they interacted with, and, in time, this would create a need for a codified form of Jewish law, based on Babylonian and Aryan codes, in the form of the Pentateuch, around 621 B.C.E.

The original excavations in the Indus produced astonishing discoveries, but this was in the time of the white, Christian-dominated era of the British Empire, and nothing that would upset the Christian perspective of history would receive very much credence or support for popular dissemination. The writings and studies concerning the value of the ancient culture were kept in the realm of the educated elite. Now that the region is under the control of fundamentalist Moslems, there is not likely to be much good news for archaeologists today. It is interesting to note that tenuous datings for Mohenjo-daro and the Aryan invasion exist on some historical timelines as 2500 B.C.E. and beginning in 2150 B.C.E., respectively, yet the fact is that there has never been a time that is known of today when the region was not inhabited and when Shiva was not worshiped. It takes historians of courage to admit that the Indus civilization actually dates back to at least 5000 B.C.E., when the Dravidians created a mythology about the Creation taking place in seven days, but they also know that the region has been actively occupied since 470,000 B.C.E., and its people worshipping Shiva since at least 28,000 B.C.E. With persistence, perhaps the censorship of historical reality will be eliminated from the education materials used in public schools.

Despite Aryan alterations, Shiva is seen today in India as a God of love (both sexual and selfless), grace, and beauty. He is the God of asceticism, and is called "Unperturbed." He does not require any religious observances or sacrifices, but simply *is*, making no demands on people and requiring no priesthood. He is the King of the Dance—Cosmic Energy in Cosmic Time. Devi, or Shakti, or Parvati, or Uma, is the Mother Goddess, the Great Goddess, the Earth Mother, and the Queen of the Universe, respectively. Together, as Ardhanari, Isha and Uma, the Lord and the Lady are One and All. This constituted the earliest form of religious veneration in Sind, Mesopotamia, and the European continent, until the advent of the new Aryan male deities invented to support a new power structure of rulers and warriors through an elite clergy. During the Aryan expansions, the religion of the Goddess and the God, lacking the addition of the political gods, was considered a threat to the new rulers of the conquered lands. Ultimately, a new religion was developed that would eliminate the lower portion of the Teutonic pyramid and declare as supreme the upper deity of the ruler. This then is the source of Judaism, and male dominance was established by the eradication of the powerful female and gentle male deities of natural religion.

When the Aryan invaders attacked the Indus Valley, they brought a patriarchal religion with them which upset the balance of nature by eliminating any real equality between the sexes. This aspect first became softened by contact with the Dravidians, then resulted in a backlash of strictness that would include the required suicide of the widow in her husband's funeral pyre. Historians are divided on whether the original Indus people buried or cremated their dead, but the various writings and archaeological finds indicate that burials occurred in the earlier history of the valley civilization, and at a later date (when the influence of the Aryans would have been felt) cremation came to displace the burial system. Among the Shivaite sects of India today, however, the traditional Dravidic burial is used. It was due to Aryan influence that Shiva was scornfully called an inhabitor of burning places, and this is the source of Satan's fiery hell for Christians, yet still the Earth Goddess (Parvati) loved Him.

The Aryans brought with them their male mountain god, who came to be viewed also as a volcano deity. Stone traces the Judaic name for God, Yahweh, to the Sanskrit for "Everflowing," and sees this as a reference to volcanic lava. The Hebrew tradition places God on His mountain, just like the God of the Northern European Aryans. The Levites were cautioned not to intermarry with any other Jewish tribe, and were authorized the best of everything the tribes had to offer. They were the priests of Yahweh, but they were also the Aryan conquerors perpetuating a caste system, just as had been done in India under the Brahmins. The same religious command that prevented the Brahmins from intermarrying with the conquered people applied to the Levites, and the wealth of the land and its people went directly to the Levites, just as it did to the Brahmins. This was only natural since they are both the same people, the Levites proudly descended from a Brahmin—Abrahm, Abraham.

The need to wipe out any trace of Shiva/Devi worship, by whatever form or name, became an Aryan imperative—much like that experienced in the actions of Hitler, which can be traced back to their inability to do so in India. Dravidic Indians fled the region and prospered in the southern part of the Indian subcontinent and Sri-Lanka (Ceylon), where Shiva is still very prominent among the Tamil populace. The modern warfare between the Tamil Hindus and Buddhists comes from the Buddhist backlash to the gentler aspects of a Shiva-dominant Hinduism. India, prior to its division by Britain into India, West Pakistan, and East Pakistan (now Bangladesh), extended from Sind eastward, and in India, Shiva could not be obliterated, but became incorporated into the pantheon along with all the aspects of His female form.

There are today different denominations of Hinduism that stress Aryan gods (Indra, Vishnu, and His incarnation as Krishna), as well as those of Shiva and Devi in all Her names and forms. This merging of deities was not tolerated by the Levite Aryans in the Middle East, and was continuously being stamped out whenever it resurfaced. Today this remains a problem in Judaism. How does the religion address the needs of women in a time when women are seeking reaffirmation of their rights and value as equal individuals with their male counterparts? Fundamentalist Christians rely on the Aryan Bible as the reason for male domination of women and actively teach women to be submissive and ruled by men (fathers, brothers, or husbands), and thus constitute a reactionary element equivalent to that of Orthodox Judaism when compared to the modern, progressive Judaism (Reformed).

This lack of status for women was not the natural state of life in pre-Christian Europe, and after the Christianization of Europe, the holdouts were labeled Pagans and Witches (the Neo-Pagan term Wiccan means "Wise One" and is sometimes considered an older usage). The Northern European Pagans had female deities whom they honored in the older, lower level of their religion, particularly in terms of fertility and the phases of the Moon, but the male deities of the upper stratum dominated.

The modern Wiccan tradition evolved from the earlier tradition of Green Witchcraft merged with the religion of the displaced Dravidians who fled from the Indus Valley in all directions, taking their God and the Goddess with them. Devi was worshiped as Danu at the time of the initial merging of the Dravidic and Aryan cultures, but subsequent waves of Aryan attackers in India saw the popular denomination as serpent demons. By this time, the Goddess was worshiped with Her Son/Consort (the Shakti aspect dominant over the Shiva aspect); and the Fertility God impregnated the Earth Goddess with Himself and was born as Her Son, indicating the seasons of the year in relation to solstices and equinoxes, and planting/harvesting times. This tradition was noted in Judaic literature and considered as "prophecy"—a promise of renewed life—and later appeared in the Christian tradition as God begetting His only Son, Himself, in the Virgin Mary (the Mother Goddess made subordinate to the Father God).

Shiva is often represented in art and sculpture with serpents (the Pagan symbols of wisdom and rebirth) in his hair and about his neck, arms, and waist. The serpent and cow were symbols of Danu during these latter Aryan invasions (circa 1500–1200 B.C.E.) when this worship was being suppressed. In Judaic mythology, Satan is described as a serpent who offers knowledge and wisdom to humankind through Eve, but when she takes the fruit of knowledge and gives it to Adam, she upsets the Aryan patriarchal deity. The priesthood could not allow people to see that immortality was a given fact of existence (energy cannot be destroyed) because this was the source of their power as intermediaries between the people and the God. In myth, they denied Adam and Eve the fruit of the Tree of Life and Knowledge, which was the gist of the Mother Goddess religion. Humanity was banished from the Garden of Eden (depicted as lying to the East—which is the location of Sind and the Indus Valley), and Shiva's bull was declared an appropriate sacrifice for the Aryan god.

Thus, the Indus followers of Danu fled to Europe and eventually to Ireland, where they are known as the Tuatha de Danu ("People of Danu"), and form part of the roots of modern Witchcraft. The Witch's heritage is that of an admixture of Celtic Pagans, Gaulic

Shiva Nataraja (Lord of the Dance)

Pagans, and Mediterranean Pagans combined with the Dravidic religion of Shiva and Shakti. The duality of the God and the Goddess is shown by the division of the modern Wiccan altar into three sections dedicated to female, both, and male (U-M-A demonstrated). The people of Sind, Dravidic and proto-Australoid, also fled in another direction and made settlements in Japan, where they were despised by the later-arriving Japanese (who originated in China) as the aboriginal Hairy Ainu (they are hairier than Orientals tend to be) and were called a white race (which would no doubt have aggravated the Aryans). Further migrations took the People of Danu across the Pacific to touch and leave their mark upon South Pacific Islands, Central and South America, and perhaps even North America, where they may have been the Anasazi Cliff Dwellers.

The modern Wiccans evolved from the migrating people called Indo-Europeans, whose belief systems incorporated some aspects of Hinduism and found expression through the European Green Wicca as well as Hindu Tantric practice and worship of the Great Goddess. When the Celtic Indo-European people, who were themselves a Dravidic derivation, met up with the earlier Tuatha de Danu, their traditions combined and the emphasis for this disenfranchised people fell on the deity of Power rather than on the deity of Grace. But the God was not ignored. Instead He became revered as Pan, Herne the Hunter, Lord of the Greenwood, and as the Green Man in his role as Tree God. He was honored as Lord of Beasts and Lord of Fertility, and these forms easily co-joined with the local prehistoric fertility religions of Europe.

As the Indo-Europeans became more settled, the God's own form of power became recognized. Shiva's Third Eye, which opens in the face of danger or enemies, flashes a powerful and destructive light that reduces the foe to ashes, and is likened to the Sun. From this, He became the Sun God of the Western Europeans. Now both God and Goddess were beings of Power and Grace, and their equality was a return to the Dravidic tradition of AUM. The God and the Goddess continued to be interchangeable in their aspects, which is sometimes confusing to newcomers to Wicca. Some people prefer to address the Goddess; others, the God—but both are the same deity, and it is wrong to suggest that only males may attune to the God and only females to the Goddess. They are both highly accessible to either sex.

Just as Atum of Egyptian tradition was the great He/She that produced Shu (Air) and Tefnut (Moisture), who then produced Nut (Goddess of the Sky) and Geb (God of the Earth), the precedent for the Hindu Atman (Self, and Adam of the Bible) dividing into male and female comes from the Dravidic source. That depiction was the

Snake Goddess

recognition by those early people that everything comes from the interaction of the principles of male and female, spirit and matter, passivity and activity. Reversal of roles is not seen as a problem, but as a means of portraying various combinations. Thus, the Earth God can be seen to interact with the Earth Goddess; the Sky God with the Sky Goddess; the Earth God with the Sky Goddess; the Earth Goddess with the Sky God. The focus can be either male or female, as with Ishtar, Queen of Heaven, and Her consort Tammuz, God of Earth; or Shiva, the Sky God, and Parvati, the Earth Goddess, and so forth.

Herein lies the basis for the differences between the Teutonic and Wiccan traditions. The Northern, Aryan Pagan source can emphasize the dominance of male deities without reference to female deities of power—a male mountain (volcano) God whose worship developed as a support for the rise of power in the chiefs and a warrior class. The Wiccan Pagan source is derived from the Southern Sind tradition which allows for an emphasis of either a female deity—a Goddess of Power and Fertility—or a male deity— a God of Grace and Fertility—but neither is whole without the other. The two Pagan traditions in Europe existed side by side until being overwhelmed by the political might of Christianity, after the Roman Emperor Constantine used the religion to hold together and control his empire. The names used in worship at the lower level of the Teutonic religious structure may differ by regions, but the symbology is the same as in Sind, and could well date back to the Indus since the valley showed signs of religious awareness some 8,000 years before Europe.

When modern African-centric professors speak of the warlike Northern Ice People and the peaceful Southern Sun People, the words are descriptive in general terms but the locations are in error. It was not Africa that brought forth the Sun People, but India. This Ice and Sun dialog represents the Aryan and Dravidic confrontation from which sprang the modern Indo-European and Near Eastern cultures. It was this blending and how it was incorporated in geographic locations that led to modern Europe and the rise of the Near Eastern states.

The Indus Valley culture was perhaps the most advanced and peaceful civilization in the early history of humankind. Like Shiva, the Unperturbed, the people seem to have been extremely tolerant of differing beliefs and ideas, and did not live under the power of any organized clergy or priesthood with attendant temples and religious bureaucracy. They appear to have been a racially integrated people who were very civic-minded and communal, were well-organized farmers, herders, and builders, had the first known urban planned cities with running water, sewers, baths, indoor restrooms, court-yards, shops, and food-dispensing warehouses. They had no temples, but followed religious practices in the privacy of the home—they were the original Solitary Practitioners (making this, then, a signifi-cantly earlier tradition than covens). And they were incredibly wealthy. When the Aryans arrived and plundered this Bronze Age people with their stronger weapons and horse-drawn chariots, the Dravidians could only give way to them a bit at a time, first the out-lying borders of Sind, then the perimeter farmsteads, then the rural villages, until at last the Aryans took it all.

It is from this remembered and drawn-out encounter (it took 950 years for the Aryans to subdue the Indus civilization) that so many of the legends of the Sidhe, or Fairie Folk, have endured. The Dravidians are the Sidhe, the Tuatha de Danu; and there can be no doubt that the tales of the fall of fabulously rich Fairie cities, the forced withdrawal of the Sidhe, the Sidhe aversion to iron, and the power of their females and Sidhe Goddess (the Fairie Queen), can all be traced to the impact of the invading Aryans on a gentle nation. So far only three major cities have been discovered in the Indus Valley, but if there is a grain of truth in legend, and in the future more large cities are found to make it a total of seven cities, they would doubtless form the basis for the Seven Cities of Gold. The quantity of riches described in the Vedas and other historical sources make that of Egypt seem poor by comparison.

When the Moslems arrived in the Indus centuries later, they were amazed at the wealth of the Hindu Brahmins. For although there was now a wretched caste system and harsh religious strictures, the nation was still rich and bountiful. The Dravidic aborigines, however, were no longer a party to the grandeur that now belonged to the Aryan conquerors, the Brahmins. The Moslems saw everything about Hinduism as an abomination to Al-Lah ("The God"—having suppressed worship of Al-Lat, "The Goddess," early on in Moslem history), and so they destroyed uncountable numbers of beautiful shrines, temples, public works, and art. They massacred hundreds of thousands of Indians, established their mosques on the sites of ancient Hindu temples and Dravidic holy places, and yet they could not destroy the Hindu religion. Instead, their actions may have encouraged the rise of Shiva worship and the subsequent "Golden Age" of Shiva in the twelfth through fifteenth centuries C.E.

The Moslem rulers confiscated land and wealth, melted down the golden statues and artworks, and destroyed the economy in a ruthless rampage that lasted until the British conquest of India. They were a raiding force that far outstripped the Aryans in ferocity and devastation, and inspired the hatred that still identifies Hindu-Moslem relations today. Even so, when the British arrived to conquer this land, the wealth of India was still a marvel. Between Aryan, Moslem, and Christian domination over India, the historical roots of religion were swept aside and often deliberately erased. Only faint clues remained as guideposts to the truth. It was too painful for arrogant Europeans to admit that the cradle of civilization was not in the Judeo-Christian-Islamic stronghold of the Near East, but on the banks of the Indus River and in the hearts of the worshippers of Shiva and Shakti.

The British bias against Indian history was typified by their habit of routinely defacing the erotic statues of the gods to make them less "offensive" to Victorian sensibilities. But perhaps it was also alarming to them to discover a similarity between the deities of the conquered Hindus and those of Britain's own Pagan past; to see that some of the classical gods of Greece and Rome may be traced back to ancient India; and to realize that prying too deeply might negate their attitude of cultural superiority. Today, one may still buy time-line maps that do not even depict India until 1500 C.E., as though the subcontinent were vacant while "superior" Western Civilization was getting started and flourishing. Such maps are still displayed in some public school rooms and many show a reference line depicting human history as beginning around 4000 B.C.E. with Adam and Eve.

The late twentieth century C.E. in America has seen the resurgence of White Supremicists, the Aryan Nation, the Ku Klux Klan, Skinheads, Neo-Nazis, and a movement to segregate the Pacific Northwest states of Oregon, Washington, Idaho, and Montana as a White Homeland. The people involved in these groups tend to claim a rigid adherence to "Christian values," particularly in the subjugation of women, the extermination of homosexuals and independent women, the dominance of the Aryan God of wrath, and the separation of the races. The intolerance and violent persecutions of nonconformists has spread from these areas into places as distant as Colorado and Maine.

The alignment of these extremist groups with the high profile Christian Fundamentalists has allowed them to see their own objectives promoted as a Christian agenda. People who support the prejudice and bigotry of the Pat Robertsons and Jerry Falwells are in effect supporting the Neo-Nazis and the White Supremicists today, just as the people of 1930s Germany and Europe did the Nazis. The first target is always the least acceptable to the majority—the mentally ill, homeless, the homosexuals, and the non-whites (Native Americans, Blacks, Vietnamese, Chinese, Indians, Pakistanis, Mexicans, and so forth), and then come the Jews, and finally the rest of the population is subjected to racial scrutiny for impure blood, to be removed through sterilization of the undesirable members of the society and imposition of marital laws. There are still laws on the books of some American states making it a crime to marry a Native American. The state of Utah, under Mormon domination, exists as a living testament to the lack of enforcement of the constitutional separation of church and state in America, and the result is a continuation of the same distortions of history taught in schools today as were taught in the days of Christian persecutions of non-Christians in Europe.

Control of people begins with small matters like "dry" counties in states whereby one set of people deny anyone else the right to buy an alcoholic beverage, to the county-wide cancellation of cable television stations that are considered too progressive, like MTV, to such mundane things as interfering in a Halloween Parade, taking children out of school for wearing a "Penguin" T-shirt (merchandise from the "Batman Returns" movie), and creating high business fees for Tarot card readers, because a rabid minority claim all these things are "Satanic" and intimidate others into agreeing lest they be called immoral. One school district nearly had to rescind its already-funded reading program in the elementary schools because of misleading propaganda from local Fundamentalist ministers accusing the program of being "Satanic" and promoting demonism and occultism. The school board, faced with a bankrupting situation, advertised and set out the controversial books for concerned parents to investigate. The highly publicized denouncements by the ministers and their congregation members led many to look over the materials. Instead of the devil and occultism, people saw funny stories and fantasy—just the sort of thing to get children interested in reading. The matter was put up to a vote on the local election ballot and the reading program was overwhelmingly accepted; but for a few weeks the community had been stirred up into a frenzy over Satanism in the schools and the local ministers received a great deal of publicity. One day the target may be the devil, the next, Peter Pan. The lists of "little" infringements would be another book, but the message here is that these things add up, and have been adding up all over the nation.

These events would be laughable except that they have an impact on people who have had no representation in the matter, and who usually have no recourse except through the individual expense of long-term court fights. The Fundamentalist ministers, however, have a tax-free monetary base, and ready access to the news media with which to organize their congregations into attack units intended to destroy the freedoms of anyone who does not conform to their dogmas. They violate the law with virtual impunity by blocking legal abortion clinics, and oppose legalizing the use in America of a successful and private contraceptive/abortion pill (RU-486) already in use in Europe. Yet the individualism and defense of private rights has been the pride of this nation. The reality is significantly different from the myth of American freedom.

As long as any group of people is able to dominate others through the codification into law of religious beliefs, the human species will remain in the Dark Ages of ignorance and superstition. That the people of Oregon rejected the 1992 attempt of Christian Fundamentalists to legally describe a segment of society in defamatory terms and as not protected under civil laws shows that there is still hope for a change in attitude; but Colorado and Maine went ahead with legalized prejudice, and the only recourse will be the Supreme Court and possibly a Constitutional Amendment. The Presidential election of 1992 did not relate to the economy or to political expression as much as it did to a nationwide rejection of the Christian Fundamentalist political incursions into the Republican Party. What happens next, only time will tell, but for people to still be fighting over the religions of Sind and Aryanism is a sad commentary on the development of the human mind and the educational system.

Today, as in the past, there is a great deal of both ethnic prejudice and nationalistic pride to overcome in rationally discussing history. Unfortunately, the evidence that ties together the religions of the human family is under threat as the cradle of civilization and religion is in the midst of Moslem Pakistan, now a Fundamentalist Islamic State. How long the artifacts of Mohenjo-daro will survive under this atmosphere is now a matter of speculation, but the region of Sind is an important site for modern Pagans and Wiccans, as well as for open-minded mainstream religionists, seeking to find a significant portion of their theological roots.

The history of the migrations of the Dravidians has entered into the mythic roots of European culture in the form of legends of the Minoans, the Etruscans, the Celts, the Fairies, the Tuatha de

Danu, and the heritage of the Eastern European Gypsies of Romania and Hungary, while the mythology of the Aryan Levites, involving numerous elements from Adam and Eve to Jesus and wicked Witches who are said to eat children, has been accepted as historical truth to the present time. Finally, however, professional archaeologists and historians are digging out and reporting significant new discoveries untainted by ecclesiastical domination. It is up to historians, scholars, and the writers of school textbooks to set history and mythology in their proper context, and it is up to educators to no longer bow to the pressure of those people who insist in perpetuating myth as history and history as myth.

Appendix A
Time Line

470,000–200,000 B.C.E.—Soan stone-age cultures in North and South Sind with Proto-Australoids and Negritos

30,000 B.C.E. —Cave paintings in Sind showing people with scimitars, swords at their waists, bows and arrows, double-headed drum, and both wild and domesticated animals

28,000 B.C.E. —Shiva, Lord of Animals cave painting

20,000 B.C.E. —European cave paintings

5000 B.C.E. —Indus myth of Creation in seven days; names for the seven days of the week; Indus city-states extend from Himalayas to Arabian Sea

4000 B.C.E. —Neolithic culture in Mysore

3600 B.C.E. —Civilization begins in Sumeria

3500 B.C.E. —Egypt's Old Kingdom

3100–2965 B.C.E. —First Egyptian dynasty

2980 B.C.E. —Egyptian accounts of famine and plenty

2900 B.C.E. —Mohenjo-daro, a thriving urban city, already very old

2872–2817 B.C.E.—Sargon I unites Sumeria and Akkad

2780 B.C.E. —First pyramid built

2700–1700 B.C.E.—Suggested as 1,000 year height of Indus

2474–2398 B.C.E.—Golden Age of Sumerian City of Ur; first Code of Laws

2375–1800 B.C.E.—Egypt's Middle Kingdom

2357 B.C.E. —Sumerian Empire destroyed by Elamites

2169–1926 B.C.E.—Babylonian Empire

2150 B.C.E. —Aryans invade outlaying area of Indus Valley (Sind) using chariots and hardened bronze weapons

2123–2081 B.C.E.—Hammurabi rules Babylon; Code of Laws

1925 B.C.E. —Aryan Hittites, armed with iron weapons, conquer Babylon

1860 B.C.E. —Stonehenge started

1800 B.C.E. —Civilization in Palestine (Canaanite)

1600 B.C.E. —Indus region falling into decline

1500 B.C.E. —Syrian poem prototype for Hebrew Daniel

1580–1100 B.C.E. —Egypt's Empire (until Dynasty of Libyan Kings); Egyptian literature prototypes for Hebrew Solomon, Lazarus, feeding multitude

1500–1200 B.C.E. —Aryans invade Indus cities in Sind;

1400 B.C.E. —Iron Age begins in India and Western Asia

1276 B.C.E. —Assyria unified

1250 B.C.E. —Mycenea falls; Canaanite cities abandoned

1232 B.C.E. —Israelite pastorialists begin new Canaanite communities on hilltops

1200 B.C.E. —Mohenjo-daro falls

1200–700 B.C.E. —Etruscans settle in Italy (named Etruria); highly civilized city-states; influenced later arriving Romans

1193 B.C.E.   —Troy destroyed by Greeks

1000–600 B.C.E. —Phoenicia and Syria Golden Age

1000–500 B.C.E. —Hindu Vedas (hymns)

900–500 B.C.E.   —Hindu Upanishads and Brahmanas, Vedas completed

884 B.C.E.   —Assyria centralized

732–609 B.C.E.   —Assyrian Empire

624–544 B.C.E.   —Life of Gautama Buddha

621 B.C.E.   —Writing of the Pentateuch (first five books of Old Testament Bible) BEGUN:

      1600–1220 B.C.E.—Alleged Egyptian Captivity

      1025–1010 B.C.E.—Saul allegedly rules Jerusalem

      1010–974 B.C.E. —David allegedly rules Jerusalem

      974–937 B.C.E.   —Solomon allegedly rules Jerusalem

      937 B.C.E.   —Jewish schism said to have created Judah and Israel

615 B.C.E.   —Jewish colonists in Egypt

609 B.C.E.   —Assyrian Empire ends

605 B.C.E.   —Egypt under Greek influence of Niku (Necho)

599–527 B.C.E.   —Jainism in India

586–538 B.C.E.   —Babylonian Captivity of Jews

559 B.C.E.   —Persian Empire under Cyrus I

539 B.C.E.   —Persian conquest of Babylon

525 B.C.E.   —Persian conquest of Egypt

520 B.C.E.   —Temple of Jerusalem built (called Second)

518 B.C.E.   —Persian invasion of India by Skylax, under Darius I

509 B.C.E.   —Roman Republic founded

500 B.C.E.   —Beginnings of Hindu orthodox system (lasts through 500 C.E.)

329 B.C.E.   —Greek invasion of India by Alexander

325 B.C.E.   —Alexander leaves India

200 B.C.E.   —Roman conquest of Etruscan city-states

138 B.C.E.   —Jewish written history starts with the Maccabees; prior to this Jerusalem was under the control of the Babylonians and Assyrians, and Israel consisted of the city and the outlying lands surrounding it

100 B.C.E.   —Images of deities in Hindu temples

                        —Cybele and Attis processions popular in Rome with Attis' death on a tree, burial in a tomb, and resurrection three days later with devotees running through the streets of Rome shouting, "He is risen!"

50 C.E.   —Images of Hindu deities with multiple arms

170 C.E.   —First attempt at creating a Christian Gospel, states that Jesus sprang from the head of God (like Athena from Zeus)

250–300 C.E.   —Christian Church becomes wealthiest religious organization in Roman Empire

300–400 C.E.   —Krishna worship spreading in India and Near East by Hindu missionaries

                        —Twelve Gospels and contents reviewed with four being selected to be "official," and three-quarters of the Gospel of Luke being discarded.

323 C.E.   —Roman Emperor Constantine declares support for Christianity and establishes the power of the Christian priesthood by so doing

400 C.E.	—Great Goddess elevated into Hindu orthodoxy; beginnings of officially accepted Tantricism
	—Shiva worship flourishing in South India and Kashmir
476 C.E.	—General date for "Fall of Roman Empire"
455–500 C.E.	—India invaded by Huns
712 C.E.	—Arab conquest of Sind (then rest of India)
900–1100 C.E.	—Shiva worship spreads to Indonesia; formal Vedic scriptures for Shiva written (the Puranas)
999–1026 C.E.	—Series of Moslem invasions and widespread looting and destruction
1100 C.E.	—Buddhism nearly extinct in India
1100–1400 C.E.	—Rise of "Heroic" Shiva
1186 C.E.	—Turkish invasion of India
1211–1236 C.E.	—Extensive Moslem control of India; and great amount of looting and destruction
1288–1293 C.E.	—Marco Polo in India
1300 C.E.	—European Renaissance just getting started
1350–1610 C.E.	—"Heroic" Shiva state religion in Mysore
1498 C.E.	—Vasco da Gama reaches India
1500–1800 C.E.	—Height of Mother Goddess worship in Bengal
1510 C.E.	—Portuguese occupy Goa, India
1525 C.E.	—Kabbalah tradition of Agrippa (1486–1535) (generally) and Paracelsus (1493–1541)
1527–1608 C.E.	—Dr. John Dee, astrologer to England's Queen Elizabeth (1558–1603)
1570–80 C.E.	—Dr. Dee develops Enochian system of ceremonial magic

1600 C.E.   —(British) East India Company founded

1756–1763 C.E.   —French-English War in India

1765 C.E.   —Robert Clive made Governor of Bengal

1858 C.E.   —British Crown takes over India

1874–1964 C.E.   —Gerald Gardner, founder Gardnerian Wicca

1877 C.E.   —Hermetic Order of the Golden Dawn estab-
                          lished by three Masons

1875–1947 C.E.   —Aleister Crowley, Ceremonial Magician

1897 C.E.   —Charles Leland wrote *Aradia,* about Italian
                          Witchcraft

1924 C.E.   —Mohenjo-daro discovered in Sind

1939 C.E.   —Gerald Gardner initiated into Witchcraft

1947 C.E.   —Britain divides India into Hindu India and
                          Moslem Pakistan (which includes the Indus
                          Valley and the archaeological sites of pre-Vedic
                          Shiva/Shakti worship)

                       —India and Pakistan independence from Britain

Appendix B
Glossary

Adept: The state acquired by an initiate into a group, particularly ceremonial magic, when material gain is no longer desired, and spiritual growth has come to such a degree that nature is at one's command.

Aesir: The Gods and Goddesses of the Warrior and Ruler levels of the Teutonic pantheon.

Anathema: Damned, detested, cursed.

Androgyne: Both male and female, a hermaphrodite; symbol of Shiva.

Ardhanari: "Half male and half female"; a name of Shiva.

Aryan: "Noble Ones"; iron-using invaders of Bronze Age India and the Near East from the North.

Asatru: "Loyal to the Aesir Gods"; a name for Odinists of the Teutonic tradition.

Asgard: Realm of the Teutonic Gods.

AUM: The sound of the name of God, with the letters meaning male, female, and both; with male emphasized, name of Shiva.

Aum namah Shivaye: "God's name is Shiva"; a mantra.

B.C.E.: "Before Common Era" or "Before Current Era"; used instead of B.C. ("Before Christ").

Bible: Compilation of religious books of Judaism and Christianity; Old Testament began with fifty-two versions circa 621 B.C.E. and orthodox version developed in which books were deleted and/or revised; New Testament began with twelve Gospels and assorted writings, with the first Book of Luke describing Jesus as having sprung from the head of God; by 400 C.E. orthodox versions edited and deleted numerous books, and deleted three-quarters of the Book of Luke.

Black Mass: Perverted celebration of Catholic Mass in which the rites were a parody of Christianity; often erroneously labeled by Christians as the same as a Witches' Sabbat.

Brahma: God of Hindu Trinity—the Creator.

Brahmin: Upper caste of Hindu society descended from the Aryan warrior-priests

Buddhism: Reformation of Hinduism to reclaim the exclusive powers of the Brahmin caste.

Caste: Hindu class distinction in four levels; Brahmins at the top and Dravidians at the bottom, and below them are the untouchables; label is hereditary, and is derived from combination of ethnic, racial, and occupational background.

C.E.: "Common Era" or "Current Era"; used instead of A.D. (Anno Domino, "Year of Our Lord").

Celts: Indo-Europeans who arrived in Ireland from the Near East by way of Spain; therefore, of Dravidic derivation.

Ceremonial Magic: Magic system based on the Kabbalah.

Coven: Group of Wiccans, usually twelve in number with one Priest or Priestess to make a total of thirteen members, although there may be two leaders, male and female.

Craft: Practice of Wicca.

Deva: "Shining Ones" of Hinduism; divine beings.

Devi: "The Goddess", name for Shakti.

Dhumavati: "Crone"; aspect of Shakti without Shiva.

Digambara: "Sky-Clad" or "Clothed in Space"; a name for Shiva.

Dravidian: Commonly used name for the early inhabitants of Mohenjo-daro and the Sind region in the Indus Valley.

Elohim: Male aspect of Judaic God, Yahweh.

Frey: "Lord"; Vanir God of lower level of Teutonic system, God of the World, animals, land, fertility, eroticism, peace and well-being, twin of Freya.

Freya: "Lady"; Vanir Goddess of lower level of Teutonic system who is able to travel to the highest level; Goddess of magic, cycles of nature, taught Odin magic, twin of Frey.

Galster: Practice of Teutonic Runic magic system.

Green Wicca: Lower level of Teutonic system, centered around Frey and Freya, natural magic/Witchcraft.

Hari: "Yellowish-green"; a name of Vishnu and reference to Krishna.

Hara: "The one who takes away"; a name of Shiva.

Heroic Shiva: Hindu reform movement seeking to re-establish equal rights for castes and women in religion and society.

Hinduism: Derivation of religious beliefs of the Dravidians of Sind and the conquering Vedic Aryans.

Indra: Vedic warrior God displaced in Hindu Trinity by Shiva.

Jaganmatri: "Divine Mother"; name for Shakti.

Jehovah: Female aspect of Judaic God, Yahweh.

Kabbalah: Supposed Jewish magical system of connections and correspondences for all aspects of the universe.

Kali: "Black"; a "terrible" aspect of Shakti, but really the passage from life to death and rebirth.

Karma: Law of retribution by which one's actions in this life dictates the nature of one's reincarnation.

Krishna: Incarnation of Vishnu, whose devotees were active missionaries in Asia Minor during time of birth of Christianity; mythological history of Krishna matches that of Jesus.

Linga: Phallic symbol of creation; emblem of Shiva.

Mahadevi: "Great Goddess"; name of Shakti.

Mantra: A chant designed to raise energy during worship of Shiva and Shakti.

Nataraja: "Lord [or King] of the Dance"; aspect of Shiva as the Cosmic Dancer.

Parvati: Earth Mother aspect of Shakti; wife of Shiva in Vedic Hinduism.

Pasupati: "Lord of the Animals"; aspect of Shiva.

Pentateuch: First five books of the Bible; the books of the Torah.

Sabbat: Wiccan celebration ritual, of which there are eight, including two solstices and two equinoxes.

Seidh: Teutonic concept of the power of magic.

Seidhr: The Practitioner of the Green level in the Teutonic system; the Green Witch.

Siddha: "Charged with energy"; occurs in Hinduism with chanting of mantras.

Sidhe: Fairie people of Ireland; the Tuatha de Danu.

Sutee: Self-immolation of widows upon the funeral pyre of their husbands.

Tantra: Complex Hindu system of practices likened to the weaving on a loom; generally emphasizes Shakti.

Tat: "That"; name for the Supreme Being in Hinduism.

Tryambaka: "Wed to the Triple Goddess"; name for Shiva.

Tuatha de Danu: "People of the Goddess Danu"; name of Dravidians in Sind during 1500–1200 B.C.E. final push of Aryans into Mohenjo-daro and name of the Sidhe, or Fairies of Ireland.

UMA: Sound of the name of God with the female aspect emphasized; name for Shakti, and for primal Goddess of Sumeria and Babylon.

Vanir: Lower level deities of Teutonic system, include worship of Frey and Freya, and practice of natural magic.

Vishnu: Second deity in Hindu Trinity; called the Preserver.

Vitki: "Wise One"; Teutonic name that became Wiccan, Witch.

Wicca: Old name for Witch; used popularly instead of Witchcraft.

Wiccan Rede: "An' it harm none, do as thou wilt"; Witches' Law.

Witchcraft: "Craft of the Wise," based generally on natural magic.

Yggdrasill: Teutonic World-Tree upon which Odin sacrificed himself by crucifixion to gain Runic magic and become King of the Gods; Aryan basis for story of Jesus' crucifixion.

Yoga: Hindu practice involving meditation and self-mortification to gain wisdom and union with the All (from which early Christians derived system of asceticism).

Yogi: One who practices Yoga.

Yoni: Vagina, or womb; symbol of Shakti as One who gives birth to all life.

Selected Bibliography

Adler, Margot. *Drawing Down the Moon: Witches, Druids, Goddess-Worshippers, and Other Pagans in America Today.* Boston: Beacon Press, 1979.

Basham, A. L. *The Wonder That Was India.* New York: Hawthorne Books, Inc., 1963.

Briggs, Katherine. *An Encyclopedia of Fairies, Hobgoblins, Brownies, Bogies, and Other Supernatural Creatures.* New York: Pantheon Books, 1976.

Burns, Ralph, Lerner, and Meacham. *World Civilizations.* Vol. C. New York: W. W. Norton & Company, Inc., 1986.

Campbell, Joseph. *The Masks of God: Primitive Mythology.* New York: Penguin Books, 1976.

_____. *The Masks of God: Oriental Mythology.* New York: Penguin Books, 1976.

Cunliffe, Barry. *The Celtic World.* New York: Greenwich House, Crown Publishers, Inc., 1986.

Danielou, Alain. *Gods of Love and Ecstasy: The Traditions of Shiva and Dionysus.* Rochester, Vermont: Inner Traditions, 1992.

Durant, Will. *The Story of Civilization: Part I, Our Oriental Heritage.* New York: Simon and Schuster, 1954.

_____. *The Story of Civilization: Part II, The Life of Greece.* New York: Simon and Schuster, 1966.

Eliot, Alexander. *The Universal Myths: Heroes, Gods, Tricksters and Others.* New York: Meridian Books, 1990.

Gibbon, Edward. *The Decline and Fall of the Roman Empire,* Vols. I & II. New York: Bennett A Cerf and Donald S. Klopper, The Modern Library, no date (mid-1940s).

Gilbert, Martin. *The Holocaust: A History of the Jews of Europe During the Second World War.* New York: Henry Holt & Company, 1985.

Goetz, Herman. *India: Five Thousand Years of Indian Art.* New York: McGraw-Hill Book Company, Inc., 1959.

González-Wippler, Migene. *The Complete Book of Spells, Ceremonies & Magic.* St. Paul: Llewellyn Publications, 1988.

Green, Marian. *A Witch Alone.* London: The Aquarian Press, 1991.

Hawkes, Jacquetta. *The First Great Civilizations: Life in Mesopotamia, the Indus Valley, and Egypt.* New York: Alfred A. Knopf, 1977.

Heyerdahl, Thor. *Aku-Aku.* New York: Rand McNally, 1958

_____. *Kon-Tiki.* New York: Rand McNally, 1950.

Holzer, Hans (introduction). *Encyclopedia of Witchcraft and Demonology.* London: BPC Publications Ltd., Octopus Books, Ltd., 1970–71.

Johari, Harish. *Tools for Tantra.* Rochester, Vermont: Inner Traditions International, Ltd., 1986.

Kersten, Holger. *Jesus Lived in India: His Unknown Life Before and After the Crucifixion.* Dorset, England: Element Book Ltd., 1986.

Klostermaier, Klaus K. *A Survey of Hinduism.* Albany: State University of New York Press, 1989.

Kramker, S. N. *The Sumerians, Their History, Culture, and Character.* Chicago: University of Chicago Press, 1963.

Kramrisch, Stella. *The Presence of Siva.* Princeton: Princeton University Press, 1981.

Legg, Stuart. *The Barbarians of Asia.* New York: Dorset Press, 1990.

Marshall, John. *Mohenjo-daro and the Indus Civilization.* 3 Vols. London: University of Oxford Press, 1931.

Massa, Aldo. *The World of the Etruscans.* Translated by John Christmas. Geneve, Italy: Minerva, 1989.

Neumayer, E. *Prehistoric India Rock Paintings.* Delhi: Oxford University Press, 1983.

O'Flaherty, Wendy Doniger. *Siva, The Erotic Ascetic.* New York: Oxford University Press, 1973.

Ross, Nancy Wilson. *Three Ways of Asian Wisdom.* New York: Simon & Schuster, 1966.

Scholem, Gershom. *Origins of the Kabbalah.* The Jewish Publication Society, Princeton University Press: 1987.

Silberman, Neil Asher. "Who Were the Israelites?" *Archaeology,* March/April, 1992.

Squire, Charles. *Celtic Myth and Legend.* Newcastle: Newcastle Publishing Co., Inc., 1975.

Starhawk. *The Spiral Dance, A Rebirth of the Ancient Religion of the Great Goddess.* New York: HarperCollins Publishers, 1989.

Stone, Merlin. *When God Was A Woman.* New York: Dorset Press, 1976.

Tacitus. *The Annals.* Book XV 36-43. Translated by Alfred John Church & William Jackson Brodribb. New York: Modern Library, 1942.

Thorsson, Edred. *Northern Magic: Mysteries of the Norse, Germans & English.* St. Paul, Minnesota: Llewellyn Publications, 1992.

Index

Adept, 37, 127, 193
Aesir, 111, 113, 119, 193
Akkad, 6, 187
Al-Lah, 61, 181
Al-Lat, 61, 181
Alexander, 17, 105, 190, 200
Ali, Mirza Husayn, 98
Anasazi, 78–79, 176
Anatolia, 42, 79, 83, 101, 115
Andhaka, 91
Androgyne, 11–12, 20, 57, 61, 68, 107, 119, 146, 163–164, 193
Anglo-Saxon(s), 27, 111–112, 120
Anti-feminism, 156
Anu, 22, 77–78
Apocrypha, 52
Aradia, 18, 122, 192
Ardhanari, 11, 20, 22–24, 61–62, 144, 163, 173, 193
Aryan(s), 4–6, 8–9, 12–17, 19–20, 22, 24, 26–28, 30–55, 57–58, 62–64, 66–68, 70–74, 77, 79–80, 82–83, 86, 90, 92–93, 97, 101–102, 104, 107, 112–120, 127, 129–132, 137–138, 140, 142, 144–154, 157–158, 164, 166–170, 172–176, 179–182, 185, 188, 193–195, 197
Aryanism, 31, 41, 62, 64, 80, 93, 107, 144, 147, 153, 167–168, 185
Asatru, 109, 120, 151–152, 157, 193
Asgard, 111, 193
Ashtoreth, 52–53, 68, 169
Asia Minor, 6, 41, 55, 64, 83, 196
Assyria, 16, 49, 188–189

Astaroth, 53, 169
Astarte, 68, 94
Attis, 11, 54, 98, 190
AUM, 19, 21, 23–25, 27, 29, 31, 33, 35, 37–38, 55, 61, 146, 163, 165, 178, 193

Babism, 98
Babylon, 3, 5, 15, 17, 43, 47, 49, 115, 163, 188–189, 197
Babylonian, 1, 14–15, 54, 169, 172, 188–189
Badb, 26
Bahai, 98
Banerji, R. D., 8
Bangledesh, 8, 18, 174
Baphomet, 80
Bathsheba, 52–53, 169
Bible, 5, 9, 12, 15–17, 43, 46–56, 58, 63–64, 67–68, 70, 72–73, 75, 80, 82, 85, 99, 129, 131–132, 147, 150, 154, 156, 168–172, 175, 178, 189, 194, 196
Black Mass, 97, 194
Brahma, 25–26, 31–33, 35–36, 59, 70, 85, 166, 194
Brahmin, 16, 32, 34, 36, 42, 174, 194
Buckland, Raymond, 123, 137
Buddha, 16, 35–36, 166, 189
Buddhism, 12, 17, 34–37, 64, 138, 191, 194
Bull, 12, 22, 30, 82, 93, 105–106, 166, 171, 176

Gay, 11
Genesis, 12, 39, 43, 47
Grace, 10–11, 24, 33, 50, 52, 63, 71,
  163, 166, 173, 178–179
Great Mother, 11, 20, 33
Great Warrior, 26, 39, 114
Green Wicca, 83, 86, 92, 97–98, 107,
  111–112, 118, 177, 195
Green Witchcraft, 112, 175
Green Witches, 112, 114–115
Gypsies, 88–89, 97, 139, 145–147,
  149, 151, 154, 185
Gypsy, 88, 97, 149

Hammurabi, 15, 43, 58, 188
Hanukkah, 28
Hara, 66, 68, 195
Harappan, 1
Hari, 66, 195
Havilah, 47
Hebrew, 15, 43, 49–50, 105, 122,
  127–128, 131, 133, 146, 154,
  171–172, 174, 188
Hecate, 26, 57, 90, 118
Hedge Witch, 112
Hermaphrodite, 11, 164, 193
Heroic Shiva, 37, 191, 195
He/She, 19, 179
Hindu, 12, 16–18, 35, 44–46, 52–53,
  59, 61, 64, 70–71, 77–79, 90–91,
  106, 128, 144, 165–166, 177–178,
  181, 189–192, 194–197
Hitler, 119–120, 145–147, 149–159,
  161, 165, 167, 169, 171, 173–175,
  177, 179, 181, 183, 185, 189
Hittites, 15, 22, 55, 116, 188
Holocaust, 9, 109, 145–147, 149, 151,
  153–155, 157, 159, 161, 165, 167,
  169, 171, 173, 175, 177, 179, 181,
  183, 185, 189, 200
Holy Land, 5, 46–47, 49, 64
Holy Rollers, 63
Homophobia, 156
Homosexual(s), 11, 19, 145–147,
  182–183

Horned God, 22, 30, 59, 80–82, 85,
  89, 91–92, 97, 101, 107, 119, 154,
  157, 166, 171
Horns, 6, 10, 80, 82, 163, 171
Hungry Face, 86
Hysterectomy, 125

India, 2–3, 6, 8–9, 12–14, 17–20, 22,
  26–27, 32, 34–35, 37–38, 40–49,
  52, 59–60, 62–68, 77–79, 83,
  88–90, 93, 97, 105–106, 123, 146,
  151–152, 163–164, 166, 169, 171,
  173–175, 180–182, 188–193,
  199–201
Indo-European, 55, 77, 118, 180
Indra, 8, 26, 60, 77, 113–114, 151,
  166, 174, 195
Indus, 1–6, 8–10, 13–17, 19–20, 22,
  24, 27, 30, 41–42, 44–49, 53, 55,
  67, 70, 77–79, 83, 89–90, 93, 101,
  104, 107, 113–116, 118, 129, 139,
  146, 149, 157, 164, 166, 169,
  172–173, 175–176, 180–182,
  187–188, 192, 195, 200–201
Industrial Revolution, 123
Insane, 62, 100, 125, 146
Ireland, 84, 90–91, 101–102, 104,
  106–107, 118, 176, 194, 196–197
Iron, 15, 102, 116, 181, 188
Ishana, 68
Ishtar, 11, 54, 68, 94, 169, 178
Ishvari, 68
Islam, 9, 46, 61, 151, 153
Israel, 17, 56, 67, 131, 150, 169,
  189–190
Israelites, 16, 42, 130–131, 172, 201

Jaganmatri, 20, 195
Jehovah, 56, 74, 195
Jerusalem, 17, 42, 47, 53, 169,
  189–190
Jesus, 5, 12, 24, 44, 48, 57–61, 63–64,
  66–67, 72, 95, 98–99, 112, 114, 142,
  167, 185, 190, 194, 196–197, 200

Judaic, 11, 41–42, 46, 48–52, 55, 63,
68, 70, 72, 82, 165–166, 169,
174–176, 195
Judaism, 9, 46, 48, 50, 53, 56, 61,
93–94, 131–133, 146, 150–151,
153, 166, 170–171, 173, 175, 194

Kabbalah, 18, 37, 110, 122, 127–128,
131–133, 137, 152, 155, 163, 165,
191, 194–195, 201
Kali, 20, 25, 57, 71, 102, 196
Karma, 63, 135, 168, 196
Karmic, 51, 135
Kashmir, 17, 44, 46–50, 59, 64, 67,
191
Knights Templar, 80
Korravai, 90
Krishna, 51, 64, 66–67, 98, 166, 174,
190, 195–196

Lawgiver, 26, 39, 41, 43, 48–49, 52,
58, 73, 120
Lazarus, 15, 43, 188
Leland, Charles, 18, 122–123, 125,
192
Levite(s), 16, 27, 42, 45, 46, 52, 53,
54, 55, 61, 62, 64, 127, 130, 131,
132, 153, 154, 171, 172, 174–175,
186
Linga, 14, 20, 28–30, 32, 37, 72, 171,
196
Lingayat, 37
Long Ears, 78
Luvite(s), 42, 55

Maccabees, 17, 52, 190
Mahabharata, 66, 118
Mahadevi, 20, 196
Manasa, 52
Mandala, 128
Mantra, 61–62, 163, 193, 196
Marshall, Sir John, 1–2, 8, 201
Mary, 22, 57–58, 67, 70–71, 154, 175

Mediterranean, 3, 5–6, 9, 16, 42, 47,
67, 79, 83–84, 86, 101, 111, 115,
129, 137, 164, 176
Mentally Ill, 145–147, 183
Mesopotamia, 1–2, 5–6, 10–11,
45–48, 50, 68, 166, 169, 173
Mises, 41, 43, 52
Mohenjo-daro, 1–3, 5–6, 8–9, 14, 34,
48, 78, 93, 101, 116, 172, 185,
187–188, 192, 195, 197, 201
Morrigu, 26, 57, 90
Moses, 9, 41, 43, 48–49, 51–52,
58–59, 70, 82
Moslem, 13–14, 17–18, 181–182, 185,
191–192
Mururgan, 90
Mycenean, 16, 42, 48, 101, 129

Nataraja, 20, 177, 196
Natural Wicca, 112
Nazi(s), 109, 120, 124, 145, 152
Nazism, 119, 149, 152
Near East, 1–2, 6, 9, 12, 14–16, 20, 22,
26–27, 41–43, 47, 49, 55, 62,
67–68, 75, 80, 83, 101, 106–107,
112–113, 144, 146, 150, 161, 172,
182, 190, 193–194
Neo-Pagan, 100, 121, 132, 134,
136–137, 151, 158, 162, 175
Neo-Paganism, 11, 74, 99, 120, 135,
138, 148, 151, 156–157, 159, 162
New Age, 137, 159
New Testament, 5, 17, 52, 60–61, 64,
68, 80, 150, 171, 194

Occultism, 125, 183–184
Odin, 26, 94, 111–113, 115, 118–120,
152, 166, 195, 197
Oestre, 94
Old Religion, 10, 53, 72, 89, 96, 99,
113, 118, 125, 136, 137, 165, 166,
171
Old Testament, 12, 43, 52–53, 58–59,
68, 80, 96, 150, 154, 171, 189, 194

STAY IN TOUCH

On the following pages you will find some of the books now available on related subjects. Your book dealer stocks most of these and will stock new titles in the Llewellyn series as they become available. We urge your patronage.

To obtain our full catalog, to keep informed about new titles as they are released, and to benefit from informative articles and helpful news, you are invited to write for our bimonthly news magazine/catalog, *Llewellyn's New Worlds of Mind and Spirit*. A sample copy is free, and it will continue coming to you at no cost as long as you are an active mail customer. Or you may subscribe for just $10.00 in the U.S.A. and Canada ($20.00 overseas, first class mail). Many bookstores also have *New Worlds* available to their customers. Ask for it.

Llewellyn's New Worlds of Mind and Spirit
P.O. Box 64383-691, St. Paul, MN 55164-0383, U.S.A.

* * *

TO ORDER BOOKS AND TAPES

If your book dealer does not have the books described, you may order them directly from the publisher by sending the full price in U.S. funds, plus $3.00 for postage and handling for orders *under* $10.00; $4.00 for orders *over* $10.00. There are no postage and handling charges for orders over $50.00. Postage and handling rates are subject to change. We ship UPS whenever possible. Delivery guaranteed. Provide your street address as UPS does not deliver to P.O. boxes. Allow 4-6 weeks for delivery. UPS to Canada requires a $50.00 minimum order. Orders outside the U.S.A. and Canada: Airmail—add retail price of book; add $5.00 for each non-book item (tapes, etc.); add $1.00 per item for surface mail.

FOR GROUP STUDY AND PURCHASE

Because there is a great deal of interest in group discussion and study of the subject matter of this book, we offer a special quantity price to group leaders or agents. Our special quantity price for a minimum order of five copies of *Dancing Shadows* is $30.00 cash-with-order. This price includes postage and handling within the United States. Minnesota residents must add 6.5% sales tax. For additional quantities, please order in multiples of five. For Canadian and foreign orders, add postage and handling charges as above. Credit card (VISA, MasterCard, American Express) orders are accepted. Charge card orders only ($15.00 minimum order) may be phoned in free within the U.S.A. or Canada by dialing 1-800-THE-MOON. For customer service, call 1-612-291-1970. Mail orders to:

LLEWELLYN PUBLICATIONS
P.O. Box 64383-691, St. Paul, MN 55164-0383, U.S.A.

Prices subject to change without notice.

GLOBAL RITUALISM
Myth & Magic Around the World
by Denny Sargent
The concept of ritual and spirituality is common to all peoples, as the same archetypal powers dwell in the psyches of people everywhere. From Haiti to Egypt, *Global Ritualism* analyzes the common themes and archetypal symbols of higher ritual so that you can define how these archetypes play out in your own life. As you build a "global vocabulary" of such spiritual and magical symbols, you will be able to construct your own vibrant, living rituals—actively following a mythos that *you* create rather than one that has been given to you.

Let the subconscious language of human archetypes become your path to spiritual evolution and meaning. Become an "eclectic ritualist" and dare to live a more fulfilling life! Includes 300 photos of actual rituals as they are enacted around the world, including 16 pages of color photos.
0-87542-700-6, 256 pgs., 271 photos, 16 color pgs., 7 x 10, softcover $19.95

LIGHT IN EXTENSION
Greek Magic from Homer to Modern Times
by David Godwin
Greek magic is the foundation of almost every form of ceremonial magic being practiced today. Elements of Greek philosophy summarize the bulk of modern esoteric thought and occult teachings. Even the cabala contains many features that appear to be Greek in origin. The systems formulated by the direct progenitors of Western culture speak to the modern soul of the Western world.

This book explains in plain, informal language the grand sweep of Greek magic and Greek philosophical and religious concepts from the archaic period of Homer's *Iliad* right down to the present. It begins with the magic and mythology of the days of classical Athens and its antecedent cultures, gives detailed considerations of Gnosticism, early Christianity and Neoplatonism—all phenomena with a Greek foundation—explains the manifestations of Greek thought in the Renaissance, and explores modern times with the Greek elements of the magic of the Golden Dawn, Aleister Crowley and others.

For the practicing magician, rituals are given that incorporate elements from each historical period that is discussed. These ceremonies may be easily adapted for Pagan or Wiccan practice or otherwise altered to suit the individual operator.

From the plains of Troy to the streets of Los Angeles, Greek magic is alive and well. No one who has any interest in magic, occultism, or hermetic thought and who is also a citizen of Western civilization can afford to ignore this heritage.
0-87542-285-3, 272 pgs., 6 x 9, illus., softcover   · $12.95